EARLY DETECTION OF CANCER USING MACHINE LEARNING

DR SURESH KUMAR RUDRAHITHLU

Dedicated to my beloved parents Late R.S.Yadapadithaya Shishila and Late Premalatha

Contents

CHAPTER ONE

Introduction

Cancer is not a single disease, but rather many related diseases that all involve uncontrolled cellular growth and reproduction. It is leading cause of death in the developed world and second in the developing world, killing almost 8 million people a year . The early diagnosis and prognosis of a cancer type have become a necessity in cancer research, as it can facilitate the subsequent clinical management of patients. For better clinical decisions, it is important to accurately distinguish between benign and malignant tumors . Conventionally, statistical methods have been used for classification of high risk and low risk cancer, despite the complex interactions of high dimensional medical data . To overcome the drawbacks of conventional statistical methods, more recently machine learning has been applied to cancer prognosis and prediction . Machine learning is a branch of artificial intelligence that employs a variety of statistical, probabilistic and optimization techniques that allows computers to "learn" from past examples and to detect hard to discern patterns from large, noisy or complex data sets . This capability is particularly well suited to medical applications, especially those that depend on complex proteomic and genomic measurements. As a result, machine learning is frequently used in cancer diagnosis and detection. This latter approach is particularly interesting as it is part of a growing trend towards personalized, predictive medicine .

A number of trends are used, including a growing dependence on protein biomarkers and microarray data, a strong bias towards applications in prostate and breast cancer, and a heavy reliance on "older" technologies such artificial neural networks (ANNs) instead of more recently developed or more easily interpretable machine learning methods. A number of published studies also I J Mutil Re App St Volume 1 Issue 1, 2017 PP. 1-8 2|Page appear to lack an appropriate level of validation or testing . Among the better designed and validated studies it is clear that machine learning methods can be used to substantially (15–25%) improve the accuracy of predicting cancer susceptibility, recurrence and mortality. At a more fundamental level, it is also evident that machine learning is also helping to improve our basic understanding of cancer development and progression . In this review different types of machine learning methods being used, the types of data being integrated and the performance of these methods in cancer prediction and prognosis.

CHALLENGES IN CLASSIFICATION OF CANCER PATIENTS The success of modern, evidence based and personalized medical research is highly dependent on the availability of a sufficient data basis in terms of quantity and quality. This often also implies topics like exchange and consolidation of data. In the area of conflict between data privacy, institutional structures and research interests, several technical, organizational and legal challenges emerge [9]. Coping with these challenges is one of the main tasks of information management in medical research. In cancer research, case study points out the marginal conditions, requirements and peculiarities of handling research data in the context of medical research .

Looking at research results, it becomes obvious that cancer diseases are more like disease families with a multitude of sub-types and that the anatomical classification of tumors might be misleading and a classification according to the pathological change of signaling pathways on the cellular level is more adequate. This differentiation is very relevant because for one patient a certain treatment may be effective and absolutely relevant while it has no positive impact on tumor control for other patients with the "same" cancer and only bears side effects .

In order to have an evidence-based medicine with a sound statistical basis, the amount and quality of available data becomes very important. The required amount of data increases with the number of relevant factors. Looking at the current cancer research, one has a vast array of factors and information—and it is still increasing . Thus, it is inevitable to cope with this heterogeneity and to

build large study bases by sharing and pooling medical research data in order to realize evidence-based personalized medicine. One way to achieve this goal could be the use of machine learning techniques. CLASSIFICATION OF MACHINE LEARNING TECHNIQUES USED IN CANCER DETECTION Recent technologies such as microarray and next-generation sequencing have paved the way for computational methods and techniques to play critical roles in this regard. Many important problems in cell biology require the dense nonlinear interactions between functional modules to be considered. The importance of computer simulation in understanding cellular processes is now widely accepted, and a variety of simulation algorithms useful for studying certain subsystems have been designed .

Cancer is not a single disease, but rather many related diseases that all involve uncontrolled cellular growth and reproduction. It is leading cause of death in the developed world and second in the developing world, killing almost 8 million people a year . The early diagnosis and prognosis of a cancer type have become a necessity in cancer research, as it can facilitate the subsequent clinical management of patients. For better clinical decisions, it is important to accurately distinguish between benign and malignant tumors . Conventionally, statistical methods have been used for classification of high risk and low risk cancer, despite the complex interactions of high dimensional medical data . To overcome the drawbacks of conventional statistical methods, more recently machine learning has been applied to cancer prognosis and prediction . Machine learning is a branch of artificial intelligence that employs a variety of statistical, probabilistic and optimization techniques that allows computers to "learn" from past examples and to detect hard to discern patterns from large, noisy or complex data sets . This capability is particularly well suited to medical applications, especially those that depend on complex proteomic and genomic measurements. As a result, machine learning is frequently used in cancer diagnosis and detection. This latter approach is particularly interesting as it is part of a growing trend towards personalized, predictive medicine .

A number of trends are used, including a growing dependence on protein biomarkers and microarray data, a strong bias towards applications in prostate and breast cancer, and a heavy reliance on "older" technologies such artificial neural networks (ANNs) instead of more recently developed or more easily interpretable machine learning methods. A number of published studies also I J Mutil Re App St Volume 1 Issue 1, 2017 PP. 1-8 2|Page appear to lack an appropriate level of validation or testing . Among the better designed and validated studies it is clear that machine learning methods can be used to substantially (15–25%) improve the accuracy of predicting cancer susceptibility, recurrence and mortality. At a more fundamental level, it is also evident that machine learning is also helping to improve our basic understanding of cancer development and progression . In this review different types of machine learning methods being used, the types of data being integrated and the performance of these methods in cancer prediction and prognosis.

CHALLENGES IN CLASSIFICATION OF CANCER PATIENTS The success of modern, evidence based and personalized medical research is highly dependent on the availability of a sufficient data basis in terms of quantity and quality. This often also implies topics like exchange and consolidation of data. In the area of conflict between data privacy, institutional structures and research interests, several technical, organizational and legal challenges emerge [9]. Coping with these challenges is one of the main tasks of information management in medical research. In cancer research, case study points out the marginal conditions, requirements and peculiarities of handling research data in the context of medical research .

Looking at research results, it becomes obvious that cancer diseases are more like disease families with a multitude of sub-types and that the anatomical classification of tumors might be misleading and a classification according to the pathological change of signaling pathways on the cellular level is more adequate. This differentiation is very relevant because for one patient a certain treatment may be effective and absolutely relevant while it has no positive impact on tumor control for other patients with the "same" cancer and only bears side effects .

In order to have an evidence-based medicine with a sound statistical basis, the amount and quality of available data becomes very important. The required amount of data increases with the number of relevant factors. Looking at the current cancer research, one has a vast array of factors and information—and it is still increasing . Thus, it is inevitable to cope with this heterogeneity and to

build large study bases by sharing and pooling medical research data in order to realize evidence-based personalized medicine. One way to achieve this goal could be the use of machine learning techniques. CLASSIFICATION OF MACHINE LEARNING TECHNIQUES USED IN CANCER DETECTION Recent technologies such as microarray and next-generation sequencing have paved the way for computational methods and techniques to play critical roles in this regard. Many important problems in cell biology require the dense nonlinear interactions between functional modules to be considered. The importance of computer simulation in understanding cellular processes is now widely accepted, and a variety of simulation algorithms useful for studying certain subsystems have been designed .

Cancer is not a single disease, but rather many related diseases that all involve uncontrolled cellular growth and reproduction. It is leading cause of death in the developed world and second in the developing world, killing almost 8 million people a year . The early diagnosis and prognosis of a cancer type have become a necessity in cancer research, as it can facilitate the subsequent clinical management of patients. For better clinical decisions, it is important to accurately distinguish between benign and malignant tumors . Conventionally, statistical methods have been used for classification of high risk and low risk cancer, despite the complex interactions of high dimensional medical data . To overcome the drawbacks of conventional statistical methods, more recently machine learning has been applied to cancer prognosis and prediction . Machine learning is a branch of artificial intelligence that employs a variety of statistical, probabilistic and optimization techniques that allows computers to "learn" from past examples and to detect hard to discern patterns from large, noisy or complex data sets . This capability is particularly well suited to medical applications, especially those that depend on complex proteomic and genomic measurements. As a result, machine learning is frequently used in cancer diagnosis and detection. This latter approach is particularly interesting as it is part of a growing trend towards personalized, predictive medicine .

A number of trends are used, including a growing dependence on protein biomarkers and microarray data, a strong bias towards applications in prostate and breast cancer, and a heavy reliance on "older" technologies such artificial neural networks (ANNs) instead of more recently developed or more easily interpretable machine learning methods. A number of published studies also I J Mutil Re App St Volume 1 Issue 1, 2017 PP. 1-8 2|Page appear to lack an appropriate level of validation or testing . Among the better designed and validated studies it is clear that machine learning methods can be used to substantially (15–25%) improve the accuracy of predicting cancer susceptibility, recurrence and mortality. At a more fundamental level, it is also evident that machine learning is also helping to improve our basic understanding of cancer development and progression . In this review different types of machine learning methods being used, the types of data being integrated and the performance of these methods in cancer prediction and prognosis.

CHALLENGES IN CLASSIFICATION OF CANCER PATIENTS The success of modern, evidence based and personalized medical research is highly dependent on the availability of a sufficient data basis in terms of quantity and quality. This often also implies topics like exchange and consolidation of data. In the area of conflict between data privacy, institutional structures and research interests, several technical, organizational and legal challenges emerge [9]. Coping with these challenges is one of the main tasks of information management in medical research. In cancer research, case study points out the marginal conditions, requirements and peculiarities of handling research data in the context of medical research .

Looking at research results, it becomes obvious that cancer diseases are more like disease families with a multitude of sub-types and that the anatomical classification of tumors might be misleading and a classification according to the pathological change of signaling pathways on the cellular level is more adequate. This differentiation is very relevant because for one patient a certain treatment may be effective and absolutely relevant while it has no positive impact on tumor control for other patients with the "same" cancer and only bears side effects .

In order to have an evidence-based medicine with a sound statistical basis, the amount and quality of available data becomes very important. The required amount of data increases with the number of relevant factors. Looking at the current cancer research, one has a vast array of factors and information—and it is still increasing . Thus, it is inevitable to cope with this heterogeneity and to

build large study bases by sharing and pooling medical research data in order to realize evidence-based personalized medicine. One way to achieve this goal could be the use of machine learning techniques. CLASSIFICATION OF MACHINE LEARNING TECHNIQUES USED IN CANCER DETECTION Recent technologies such as microarray and next-generation sequencing have paved the way for computational methods and techniques to play critical roles in this regard. Many important problems in cell biology require the dense nonlinear interactions between functional modules to be considered. The importance of computer simulation in understanding cellular processes is now widely accepted, and a variety of simulation algorithms useful for studying certain subsystems have been designed .

Cancer is not a single disease, but rather many related diseases that all involve uncontrolled cellular growth and reproduction. It is leading cause of death in the developed world and second in the developing world, killing almost 8 million people a year . The early diagnosis and prognosis of a cancer type have become a necessity in cancer research, as it can facilitate the subsequent clinical management of patients. For better clinical decisions, it is important to accurately distinguish between benign and malignant tumors . Conventionally, statistical methods have been used for classification of high risk and low risk cancer, despite the complex interactions of high dimensional medical data . To overcome the drawbacks of conventional statistical methods, more recently machine learning has been applied to cancer prognosis and prediction . Machine learning is a branch of artificial intelligence that employs a variety of statistical, probabilistic and optimization techniques that allows computers to "learn" from past examples and to detect hard to discern patterns from large, noisy or complex data sets . This capability is particularly well suited to medical applications, especially those that depend on complex proteomic and genomic measurements. As a result, machine learning is frequently used in cancer diagnosis and detection. This latter approach is particularly interesting as it is part of a growing trend towards personalized, predictive medicine .

A number of trends are used, including a growing dependence on protein biomarkers and microarray data, a strong bias towards applications in prostate and breast cancer, and a heavy reliance on "older" technologies such artificial neural networks (ANNs) instead of more recently developed or more easily interpretable machine learning methods. A number of published studies also I J Mutil Re App St Volume 1 Issue 1, 2017 PP. 1-8 2|Page appear to lack an appropriate level of validation or testing . Among the better designed and validated studies it is clear that machine learning methods can be used to substantially (15–25%) improve the accuracy of predicting cancer susceptibility, recurrence and mortality. At a more fundamental level, it is also evident that machine learning is also helping to improve our basic understanding of cancer development and progression . In this review different types of machine learning methods being used, the types of data being integrated and the performance of these methods in cancer prediction and prognosis.

CHALLENGES IN CLASSIFICATION OF CANCER PATIENTS The success of modern, evidence based and personalized medical research is highly dependent on the availability of a sufficient data basis in terms of quantity and quality. This often also implies topics like exchange and consolidation of data. In the area of conflict between data privacy, institutional structures and research interests, several technical, organizational and legal challenges emerge [9]. Coping with these challenges is one of the main tasks of information management in medical research. In cancer research, case study points out the marginal conditions, requirements and peculiarities of handling research data in the context of medical research .

Looking at research results, it becomes obvious that cancer diseases are more like disease families with a multitude of sub-types and that the anatomical classification of tumors might be misleading and a classification according to the pathological change of signaling pathways on the cellular level is more adequate. This differentiation is very relevant because for one patient a certain treatment may be effective and absolutely relevant while it has no positive impact on tumor control for other patients with the "same" cancer and only bears side effects .

In order to have an evidence-based medicine with a sound statistical basis, the amount and quality of available data becomes very important. The required amount of data increases with the number of relevant factors. Looking at the current cancer research, one has a vast array of factors and information—and it is still increasing . Thus, it is inevitable to cope with this heterogeneity and to

build large study bases by sharing and pooling medical research data in order to realize evidence-based personalized medicine. One way to achieve this goal could be the use of machine learning techniques. CLASSIFICATION OF MACHINE LEARNING TECHNIQUES USED IN CANCER DETECTION Recent technologies such as microarray and next-generation sequencing have paved the way for computational methods and techniques to play critical roles in this regard. Many important problems in cell biology require the dense nonlinear interactions between functional modules to be considered. The importance of computer simulation in understanding cellular processes is now widely accepted, and a variety of simulation algorithms useful for studying certain subsystems have been designed .

Cancer is not a single disease, but rather many related diseases that all involve uncontrolled cellular growth and reproduction. It is leading cause of death in the developed world and second in the developing world, killing almost 8 million people a year . The early diagnosis and prognosis of a cancer type have become a necessity in cancer research, as it can facilitate the subsequent clinical management of patients. For better clinical decisions, it is important to accurately distinguish between benign and malignant tumors . Conventionally, statistical methods have been used for classification of high risk and low risk cancer, despite the complex interactions of high dimensional medical data . To overcome the drawbacks of conventional statistical methods, more recently machine learning has been applied to cancer prognosis and prediction . Machine learning is a branch of artificial intelligence that employs a variety of statistical, probabilistic and optimization techniques that allows computers to "learn" from past examples and to detect hard to discern patterns from large, noisy or complex data sets . This capability is particularly well suited to medical applications, especially those that depend on complex proteomic and genomic measurements. As a result, machine learning is frequently used in cancer diagnosis and detection. This latter approach is particularly interesting as it is part of a growing trend towards personalized, predictive medicine .

A number of trends are used, including a growing dependence on protein biomarkers and microarray data, a strong bias towards applications in prostate and breast cancer, and a heavy reliance on "older" technologies such artificial neural networks (ANNs) instead of more recently developed or more easily interpretable machine learning methods. A number of published studies also I J Mutil Re App St Volume 1 Issue 1, 2017 PP. 1-8 2|Page appear to lack an appropriate level of validation or testing . Among the better designed and validated studies it is clear that machine learning methods can be used to substantially (15–25%) improve the accuracy of predicting cancer susceptibility, recurrence and mortality. At a more fundamental level, it is also evident that machine learning is also helping to improve our basic understanding of cancer development and progression . In this review different types of machine learning methods being used, the types of data being integrated and the performance of these methods in cancer prediction and prognosis.

CHALLENGES IN CLASSIFICATION OF CANCER PATIENTS The success of modern, evidence based and personalized medical research is highly dependent on the availability of a sufficient data basis in terms of quantity and quality. This often also implies topics like exchange and consolidation of data. In the area of conflict between data privacy, institutional structures and research interests, several technical, organizational and legal challenges emerge [9]. Coping with these challenges is one of the main tasks of information management in medical research. In cancer research, case study points out the marginal conditions, requirements and peculiarities of handling research data in the context of medical research .

Looking at research results, it becomes obvious that cancer diseases are more like disease families with a multitude of sub-types and that the anatomical classification of tumors might be misleading and a classification according to the pathological change of signaling pathways on the cellular level is more adequate. This differentiation is very relevant because for one patient a certain treatment may be effective and absolutely relevant while it has no positive impact on tumor control for other patients with the "same" cancer and only bears side effects .

In order to have an evidence-based medicine with a sound statistical basis, the amount and quality of available data becomes very important. The required amount of data increases with the number of relevant factors. Looking at the current cancer research, one has a vast array of factors and information—and it is still increasing . Thus, it is inevitable to cope with this heterogeneity and to

build large study bases by sharing and pooling medical research data in order to realize evidence-based personalized medicine. One way to achieve this goal could be the use of machine learning techniques. CLASSIFICATION OF MACHINE LEARNING TECHNIQUES USED IN CANCER DETECTION Recent technologies such as microarray and next-generation sequencing have paved the way for computational methods and techniques to play critical roles in this regard. Many important problems in cell biology require the dense nonlinear interactions between functional modules to be considered. The importance of computer simulation in understanding cellular processes is now widely accepted, and a variety of simulation algorithms useful for studying certain subsystems have been designed .

Cancer is not a single disease, but rather many related diseases that all involve uncontrolled cellular growth and reproduction. It is leading cause of death in the developed world and second in the developing world, killing almost 8 million people a year . The early diagnosis and prognosis of a cancer type have become a necessity in cancer research, as it can facilitate the subsequent clinical management of patients. For better clinical decisions, it is important to accurately distinguish between benign and malignant tumors . Conventionally, statistical methods have been used for classification of high risk and low risk cancer, despite the complex interactions of high dimensional medical data . To overcome the drawbacks of conventional statistical methods, more recently machine learning has been applied to cancer prognosis and prediction . Machine learning is a branch of artificial intelligence that employs a variety of statistical, probabilistic and optimization techniques that allows computers to "learn" from past examples and to detect hard to discern patterns from large, noisy or complex data sets . This capability is particularly well suited to medical applications, especially those that depend on complex proteomic and genomic measurements. As a result, machine learning is frequently used in cancer diagnosis and detection. This latter approach is particularly interesting as it is part of a growing trend towards personalized, predictive medicine .

A number of trends are used, including a growing dependence on protein biomarkers and microarray data, a strong bias towards applications in prostate and breast cancer, and a heavy reliance on "older" technologies such artificial neural networks (ANNs) instead of more recently developed or more easily interpretable machine learning methods. A number of published studies also I J Mutil Re App St Volume 1 Issue 1, 2017 PP. 1-8 2|Page appear to lack an appropriate level of validation or testing . Among the better designed and validated studies it is clear that machine learning methods can be used to substantially (15–25%) improve the accuracy of predicting cancer susceptibility, recurrence and mortality. At a more fundamental level, it is also evident that machine learning is also helping to improve our basic understanding of cancer development and progression . In this review different types of machine learning methods being used, the types of data being integrated and the performance of these methods in cancer prediction and prognosis.

CHALLENGES IN CLASSIFICATION OF CANCER PATIENTS The success of modern, evidence based and personalized medical research is highly dependent on the availability of a sufficient data basis in terms of quantity and quality. This often also implies topics like exchange and consolidation of data. In the area of conflict between data privacy, institutional structures and research interests, several technical, organizational and legal challenges emerge [9]. Coping with these challenges is one of the main tasks of information management in medical research. In cancer research, case study points out the marginal conditions, requirements and peculiarities of handling research data in the context of medical research .

Looking at research results, it becomes obvious that cancer diseases are more like disease families with a multitude of sub-types and that the anatomical classification of tumors might be misleading and a classification according to the pathological change of signaling pathways on the cellular level is more adequate. This differentiation is very relevant because for one patient a certain treatment may be effective and absolutely relevant while it has no positive impact on tumor control for other patients with the “same” cancer and only bears side effects .

In order to have an evidence-based medicine with a sound statistical basis, the amount and quality of available data becomes very important. The required amount of data increases with the number of relevant factors. Looking at the current cancer research, one has a vast array of factors and information—and it is still increasing . Thus, it is inevitable to cope with this heterogeneity and to

build large study bases by sharing and pooling medical research data in order to realize evidence-based personalized medicine. One way to achieve this goal could be the use of machine learning techniques. CLASSIFICATION OF MACHINE LEARNING TECHNIQUES USED IN CANCER DETECTION Recent technologies such as microarray and next-generation sequencing have paved the way for computational methods and techniques to play critical roles in this regard. Many important problems in cell biology require the dense nonlinear interactions between functional modules to be considered. The importance of computer simulation in understanding cellular processes is now widely accepted, and a variety of simulation algorithms useful for studying certain subsystems have been designed .

Cancer is not a single disease, but rather many related diseases that all involve uncontrolled cellular growth and reproduction. It is leading cause of death in the developed world and second in the developing world, killing almost 8 million people a year . The early diagnosis and prognosis of a cancer type have become a necessity in cancer research, as it can facilitate the subsequent clinical management of patients. For better clinical decisions, it is important to accurately distinguish between benign and malignant tumors . Conventionally, statistical methods have been used for classification of high risk and low risk cancer, despite the complex interactions of high dimensional medical data . To overcome the drawbacks of conventional statistical methods, more recently machine learning has been applied to cancer prognosis and prediction . Machine learning is a branch of artificial intelligence that employs a variety of statistical, probabilistic and optimization techniques that allows computers to “learn” from past examples and to detect hard to discern patterns from large, noisy or complex data sets . This capability is particularly well suited to medical applications, especially those that depend on complex proteomic and genomic measurements. As a result, machine learning is frequently used in cancer diagnosis and detection. This latter approach is particularly interesting as it is part of a growing trend towards personalized, predictive medicine .

A number of trends are used, including a growing dependence on protein biomarkers and microarray data, a strong bias towards applications in prostate and breast cancer, and a heavy reliance on “older” technologies such artificial neural networks (ANNs) instead of more recently developed or more easily interpretable machine learning methods. A number of published studies also I J Mutil Re App St Volume 1 Issue 1, 2017 PP. 1-8 2|Page appear to lack an appropriate level of validation or testing . Among the better designed and validated studies it is clear that machine learning methods can be used to substantially (15–25%) improve the accuracy of predicting cancer susceptibility, recurrence and mortality. At a more fundamental level, it is also evident that machine learning is also helping to improve our basic understanding of cancer development and progression . In this review different types of machine learning methods being used, the types of data being integrated and the performance of these methods in cancer prediction and prognosis.

CHALLENGES IN CLASSIFICATION OF CANCER PATIENTS The success of modern, evidence based and personalized medical research is highly dependent on the availability of a sufficient data basis in terms of quantity and quality. This often also implies topics like exchange and consolidation of data. In the area of conflict between data privacy, institutional structures and research interests, several technical, organizational and legal challenges emerge [9]. Coping with these challenges is one of the main tasks of information management in medical research. In cancer research, case study points out the marginal conditions, requirements and peculiarities of handling research data in the context of medical research .

Looking at research results, it becomes obvious that cancer diseases are more like disease families with a multitude of sub-types and that the anatomical classification of tumors might be misleading and a classification according to the pathological change of signaling pathways on the cellular level is more adequate. This differentiation is very relevant because for one patient a certain treatment may be effective and absolutely relevant while it has no positive impact on tumor control for other patients with the "same" cancer and only bears side effects .

In order to have an evidence-based medicine with a sound statistical basis, the amount and quality of available data becomes very important. The required amount of data increases with the number of relevant factors. Looking at the current cancer research, one has a vast array of factors and information—and it is still increasing . Thus, it is inevitable to cope with this heterogeneity and to

build large study bases by sharing and pooling medical research data in order to realize evidence-based personalized medicine. One way to achieve this goal could be the use of machine learning techniques. CLASSIFICATION OF MACHINE LEARNING TECHNIQUES USED IN CANCER DETECTION Recent technologies such as microarray and next-generation sequencing have paved the way for computational methods and techniques to play critical roles in this regard. Many important problems in cell biology require the dense nonlinear interactions between functional modules to be considered. The importance of computer simulation in understanding cellular processes is now widely accepted, and a variety of simulation algorithms useful for studying certain subsystems have been designed .

Cancer is not a single disease, but rather many related diseases that all involve uncontrolled cellular growth and reproduction. It is leading cause of death in the developed world and second in the developing world, killing almost 8 million people a year . The early diagnosis and prognosis of a cancer type have become a necessity in cancer research, as it can facilitate the subsequent clinical management of patients. For better clinical decisions, it is important to accurately distinguish between benign and malignant tumors . Conventionally, statistical methods have been used for classification of high risk and low risk cancer, despite the complex interactions of high dimensional medical data . To overcome the drawbacks of conventional statistical methods, more recently machine learning has been applied to cancer prognosis and prediction . Machine learning is a branch of artificial intelligence that employs a variety of statistical, probabilistic and optimization techniques that allows computers to "learn" from past examples and to detect hard to discern patterns from large, noisy or complex data sets . This capability is particularly well suited to medical applications, especially those that depend on complex proteomic and genomic measurements. As a result, machine learning is frequently used in cancer diagnosis and detection. This latter approach is particularly interesting as it is part of a growing trend towards personalized, predictive medicine .

A number of trends are used, including a growing dependence on protein biomarkers and microarray data, a strong bias towards applications in prostate and breast cancer, and a heavy reliance on "older" technologies such artificial neural networks (ANNs) instead of more recently developed or more easily interpretable machine learning methods. A number of published studies also I J Mutil Re App St Volume 1 Issue 1, 2017 PP. 1-8 2|Page appear to lack an appropriate level of validation or testing . Among the better designed and validated studies it is clear that machine learning methods can be used to substantially (15–25%) improve the accuracy of predicting cancer susceptibility, recurrence and mortality. At a more fundamental level, it is also evident that machine learning is also helping to improve our basic understanding of cancer development and progression . In this review different types of machine learning methods being used, the types of data being integrated and the performance of these methods in cancer prediction and prognosis.

CHALLENGES IN CLASSIFICATION OF CANCER PATIENTS The success of modern, evidence based and personalized medical research is highly dependent on the availability of a sufficient data basis in terms of quantity and quality. This often also implies topics like exchange and consolidation of data. In the area of conflict between data privacy, institutional structures and research interests, several technical, organizational and legal challenges emerge [9]. Coping with these challenges is one of the main tasks of information management in medical research. In cancer research, case study points out the marginal conditions, requirements and peculiarities of handling research data in the context of medical research .

Looking at research results, it becomes obvious that cancer diseases are more like disease families with a multitude of sub-types and that the anatomical classification of tumors might be misleading and a classification according to the pathological change of signaling pathways on the cellular level is more adequate. This differentiation is very relevant because for one patient a certain treatment may be effective and absolutely relevant while it has no positive impact on tumor control for other patients with the "same" cancer and only bears side effects .

In order to have an evidence-based medicine with a sound statistical basis, the amount and quality of available data becomes very important. The required amount of data increases with the number of relevant factors. Looking at the current cancer research, one has a vast array of factors and information—and it is still increasing . Thus, it is inevitable to cope with this heterogeneity and to

build large study bases by sharing and pooling medical research data in order to realize evidence-based personalized medicine. One way to achieve this goal could be the use of machine learning techniques. CLASSIFICATION OF MACHINE LEARNING TECHNIQUES USED IN CANCER DETECTION Recent technologies such as microarray and next-generation sequencing have paved the way for computational methods and techniques to play critical roles in this regard. Many important problems in cell biology require the dense nonlinear interactions between functional modules to be considered. The importance of computer simulation in understanding cellular processes is now widely accepted, and a variety of simulation algorithms useful for studying certain subsystems have been designed .

Cancer is not a single disease, but rather many related diseases that all involve uncontrolled cellular growth and reproduction. It is leading cause of death in the developed world and second in the developing world, killing almost 8 million people a year . The early diagnosis and prognosis of a cancer type have become a necessity in cancer research, as it can facilitate the subsequent clinical management of patients. For better clinical decisions, it is important to accurately distinguish between benign and malignant tumors . Conventionally, statistical methods have been used for classification of high risk and low risk cancer, despite the complex interactions of high dimensional medical data . To overcome the drawbacks of conventional statistical methods, more recently machine learning has been applied to cancer prognosis and prediction . Machine learning is a branch of artificial intelligence that employs a variety of statistical, probabilistic and optimization techniques that allows computers to "learn" from past examples and to detect hard to discern patterns from large, noisy or complex data sets . This capability is particularly well suited to medical applications, especially those that depend on complex proteomic and genomic measurements. As a result, machine learning is frequently used in cancer diagnosis and detection. This latter approach is particularly interesting as it is part of a growing trend towards personalized, predictive medicine .

A number of trends are used, including a growing dependence on protein biomarkers and microarray data, a strong bias towards applications in prostate and breast cancer, and a heavy reliance on "older" technologies such artificial neural networks (ANNs) instead of more recently developed or more easily interpretable machine learning methods. A number of published studies also I J Mutil Re App St Volume 1 Issue 1, 2017 PP. 1-8 2|Page appear to lack an appropriate level of validation or testing . Among the better designed and validated studies it is clear that machine learning methods can be used to substantially (15–25%) improve the accuracy of predicting cancer susceptibility, recurrence and mortality. At a more fundamental level, it is also evident that machine learning is also helping to improve our basic understanding of cancer development and progression . In this review different types of machine learning methods being used, the types of data being integrated and the performance of these methods in cancer prediction and prognosis.

CHALLENGES IN CLASSIFICATION OF CANCER PATIENTS The success of modern, evidence based and personalized medical research is highly dependent on the availability of a sufficient data basis in terms of quantity and quality. This often also implies topics like exchange and consolidation of data. In the area of conflict between data privacy, institutional structures and research interests, several technical, organizational and legal challenges emerge [9]. Coping with these challenges is one of the main tasks of information management in medical research. In cancer research, case study points out the marginal conditions, requirements and peculiarities of handling research data in the context of medical research .

Looking at research results, it becomes obvious that cancer diseases are more like disease families with a multitude of sub-types and that the anatomical classification of tumors might be misleading and a classification according to the pathological change of signaling pathways on the cellular level is more adequate. This differentiation is very relevant because for one patient a certain treatment may be effective and absolutely relevant while it has no positive impact on tumor control for other patients with the "same" cancer and only bears side effects .

In order to have an evidence-based medicine with a sound statistical basis, the amount and quality of available data becomes very important. The required amount of data increases with the number of relevant factors. Looking at the current cancer research, one has a vast array of factors and information—and it is still increasing . Thus, it is inevitable to cope with this heterogeneity and to

build large study bases by sharing and pooling medical research data in order to realize evidence-based personalized medicine. One way to achieve this goal could be the use of machine learning techniques. CLASSIFICATION OF MACHINE LEARNING TECHNIQUES USED IN CANCER DETECTION Recent technologies such as microarray and next-generation sequencing have paved the way for computational methods and techniques to play critical roles in this regard. Many important problems in cell biology require the dense nonlinear interactions between functional modules to be considered. The importance of computer simulation in understanding cellular processes is now widely accepted, and a variety of simulation algorithms useful for studying certain subsystems have been designed .

Cancer is not a single disease, but rather many related diseases that all involve uncontrolled cellular growth and reproduction. It is leading cause of death in the developed world and second in the developing world, killing almost 8 million people a year . The early diagnosis and prognosis of a cancer type have become a necessity in cancer research, as it can facilitate the subsequent clinical management of patients. For better clinical decisions, it is important to accurately distinguish between benign and malignant tumors . Conventionally, statistical methods have been used for classification of high risk and low risk cancer, despite the complex interactions of high dimensional medical data . To overcome the drawbacks of conventional statistical methods, more recently machine learning has been applied to cancer prognosis and prediction . Machine learning is a branch of artificial intelligence that employs a variety of statistical, probabilistic and optimization techniques that allows computers to "learn" from past examples and to detect hard to discern patterns from large, noisy or complex data sets . This capability is particularly well suited to medical applications, especially those that depend on complex proteomic and genomic measurements. As a result, machine learning is frequently used in cancer diagnosis and detection. This latter approach is particularly interesting as it is part of a growing trend towards personalized, predictive medicine .

A number of trends are used, including a growing dependence on protein biomarkers and microarray data, a strong bias towards applications in prostate and breast cancer, and a heavy reliance on "older" technologies such artificial neural networks (ANNs) instead of more recently developed or more easily interpretable machine learning methods. A number of published studies also I J Mutil Re App St Volume 1 Issue 1, 2017 PP. 1-8 2|Page appear to lack an appropriate level of validation or testing . Among the better designed and validated studies it is clear that machine learning methods can be used to substantially (15–25%) improve the accuracy of predicting cancer susceptibility, recurrence and mortality. At a more fundamental level, it is also evident that machine learning is also helping to improve our basic understanding of cancer development and progression . In this review different types of machine learning methods being used, the types of data being integrated and the performance of these methods in cancer prediction and prognosis.

CHALLENGES IN CLASSIFICATION OF CANCER PATIENTS The success of modern, evidence based and personalized medical research is highly dependent on the availability of a sufficient data basis in terms of quantity and quality. This often also implies topics like exchange and consolidation of data. In the area of conflict between data privacy, institutional structures and research interests, several technical, organizational and legal challenges emerge [9]. Coping with these challenges is one of the main tasks of information management in medical research. In cancer research, case study points out the marginal conditions, requirements and peculiarities of handling research data in the context of medical research .

Looking at research results, it becomes obvious that cancer diseases are more like disease families with a multitude of sub-types and that the anatomical classification of tumors might be misleading and a classification according to the pathological change of signaling pathways on the cellular level is more adequate. This differentiation is very relevant because for one patient a certain treatment may be effective and absolutely relevant while it has no positive impact on tumor control for other patients with the "same" cancer and only bears side effects .

In order to have an evidence-based medicine with a sound statistical basis, the amount and quality of available data becomes very important. The required amount of data increases with the number of relevant factors. Looking at the current cancer research, one has a vast array of factors and information—and it is still increasing . Thus, it is inevitable to cope with this heterogeneity and to

build large study bases by sharing and pooling medical research data in order to realize evidence-based personalized medicine. One way to achieve this goal could be the use of machine learning techniques. CLASSIFICATION OF MACHINE LEARNING TECHNIQUES USED IN CANCER DETECTION Recent technologies such as microarray and next-generation sequencing have paved the way for computational methods and techniques to play critical roles in this regard. Many important problems in cell biology require the dense nonlinear interactions between functional modules to be considered. The importance of computer simulation in understanding cellular processes is now widely accepted, and a variety of simulation algorithms useful for studying certain subsystems have been designed .

CHAPTER TWO

Early detection of Cancer using Machine Learning

In machine learning method, data and output is run on the computer to create a program :

1. Sparse compact incremental learning machine (SCILM) method A new approach was designed to resolve cancer classification problem on microarray gene expression data, which take advantage of correntropy cost that makes it robust against diverse noises and outliers. Moreover, since SCILM uses l1-norm of the weights, it has sparseness, which can be applied for gene selection purposes as well. Finally, due to compact structure, the method is capable of performing classification tasks in all of the cases with only one neuron in its hidden layer. The experimental analysis in this method was performed on 26 well-known microarray data sets regarding diverse kinds of cancers and the results showed that the strategy not only achieved significantly high accuracy but also accompanied with effectivity of each gene regarding the corresponding cancer .

2. Knowledge base system learning method A new knowledge-based system for classification of cancer disease was proposed using clustering, noise removal, and classification techniques. Expectation Maximization (EM) was used as a clustering method to cluster the data in similar groups. Classification and Regression Trees (CART) were used to generate the fuzzy rules to be used for the classification of cancer disease in the knowledge-based system of fuzzy rule-based reasoning method. To overcome the multicollinearity issue, Principal Component Analysis (PCA) was incorporated in the current knowledge-based system. Experimental results on Wisconsin Diagnostic Breast Cancer and Mammographic mass datasets showed that current approach remarkably improves the prediction accuracy of breast cancer. The knowledge-based system can be used .

3. Gauss-Newton representation based learning method A novel Gauss-Newton representation based algorithm (GNRBA) for breast cancer classification. It uses the sparse representation with training sample selection. Until now, sparse representation has been successfully applied in pattern recognition only. This method introduces a novel Gauss-Newton based approach to find the optimal weights for the training samples for classification. In addition, it evaluates the sparsity in a computationally efficient way as compared to the conventional l1-norm method. The effectiveness of the GNRBA is examined on the Wisconsin Breast Cancer Database (WBCD) and

the Wisconsin Diagnosis Breast Cancer (WDBC) database from the UCI Machine Learning repository. Various performance measures like classification accuracy, sensitivity, specificity, confusion matrices, a statistical test and the area under the receiver operating characteristic (AUC) are reported to show the superiority of the proposed method as compared to classical models [17].

4. Gene expression learning method Studying the characteristics of thousands of genes simultaneously offered a deep insight into cancer classification problem. It introduced an abundant amount of data ready to be explored. It has also been applied in a wide range of applications such as drug discovery, cancer prediction and diagnosis which is a very important issue for cancer treatment . Besides, it helps in understanding the function of genes and the interaction between genes in

normal and abnormal conditions . That is done by monitoring the behavior of genes, gene expression data under different conditions. Ensemble classifiers increase not only the performance of the classification, but also the confidence of the results. The motivations beyond using ensemble classifiers are that the results are less dependent on peculiarities of a single training set and because the ensemble system outperforms the performance of the best base classifier in the ensemble [19].

5. Ensemble predictive modeling framework learning method Molecular changes often precede clinical presentation of diseases and can be useful surrogates with potential to assist in informed clinical decision making. Recent studies have demonstrated the usefulness of modeling approaches such as classification that can predict the clinical outcomes from molecular expression profiles. While useful, a majority of these approaches implicitly use all molecular markers as features in the classification process often resulting in sparse high-dimensional projection of the samples often comparable to that of the sample size. Ensemble classification approach is used for predicting good and poorprognosis breast cancer samples from their molecular expression profiles [20]. In contrast to traditional single and ensemble classifiers, the proposed approach uses multiple base classifiers with varying feature sets obtained from two-dimensional projection of the samples in conjunction with a majority voting strategy for predicting the class labels .

In contrast to earlier implementation, base classifiers in the ensembles are chosen based on maximal sensitivity and minimal redundancy by choosing only those with low average cosine distance. The resulting ensemble sets are subsequently modeled as undirected graphs. Performance of four different classification algorithms is shown to be better within the proposed ensemble framework in contrast to using them as traditional single classifier systems. Design of an efficient ensemble predictive modeling classification framework for prediction of breast density class .

6. Convolution neural network learning method Deep convolutional neural networks (CNNs) were designed to obtain more discriminative description of cancer tissues. Benefiting from the discriminative representation, metric learning layers are proposed to further improve performance of the deep structure. The bestperforming model restricts the depth of back I J Mutil Re App St Volume 1 Issue 1, 2017 PP. 1-8 6|Page propagation of joint training in only the metric learning layers. Relation between metric learning layers and tradition CNNs structures seems like parasitism relationship between species, where one species, the parasite, benefits at the expense of the other .

Therefore, the method is named as parasitic metric learning net. To confirm veracity of this method, classification experiments on breast mass images of two widely used databases were performed . Comparing performance of the current method with traditional ones, competitive results were achieved. Meanwhile, the parameter updating strategy for parasitic metric net may inspire a way of improving performance of a pre-trained CNNs model on particular medical image processing or other computer vision tasks . Training pipeline of the proposed parasitic metric learning net .We discussed the concepts of machine learning while we outlined their application in cancer prediction/prognosis. Most of the studies that have been proposed the last years and focus on the development of predictive models using supervised machine learning methods and classification algorithms aiming to predict valid disease outcomes. Based on the analysis of their results, it is evident that the integration of multidimensional heterogeneous data, combined with the application of different techniques for feature selection and classification can provide promising tools for inference in the cancer domain.

EXPERIMENT AND METHODOLOGY :.

1 Data-sets A malignant tumour that has developed from cells of the breast is breast cancer. Although some of the scientifically known risk factors (i.e. ageing, genetic risk factors, family history, menstrual periods, not having children, obesity) that increase a woman's chance of developing breast cancer, the exact causes or some of these risk factors that causes cells to become cancerous are not exactly known by them. Research is under way to learn more and scientists are making great progress in understanding how certain changes in DNA can cause normal breast cells to become cancerous. This part of the project includes the research about the available dataset that can be used for the project. The initial dataset that we planned on working had certain drawbacks. CBIS-DDSM dataset: Neither the analytics nor the experimental validation of the data were sufficient to move forward with the project. There was no exact data regarding the classification of tumours into benign and malignant in case of scan images of patients. One the most important demerit of this dataset was the improper organization of data and huge redundant records which can cause glitches in the training process. Hence it was concluded that evaluation based on detection rate and accuracy levels with this data-set is not appropriate. Breast cancer Wisconsin data-set: This dataset was a text type data-set which had a classified set of data into malignant and benign tumours based on the cell features threshold values for various features like cell radius, perimeter, area, symmetry and other such International Research Journal of Engineering and Technology . We didn't go for this data-set since we planned on a better version of cancer detection model which focused on images

2 Pre-processing data Data preprocessing is a data mining technique that is used for filter data in a usable format. Because the real-world data-set is almost available in different formats. It's not available as per our requirement so it must fit the data-set in an understandable format. Data pre processing is a proven method of resolving such issues. Data pre-processing converts the data-set into usable format for pre-processing. We have used a standardization method to pre- process the data-set. Encoder Method: Label Encoder is an efficient tool for encoding the levels of the categorical features into numeric values. Label Encoder encode labels with value between 0 and classes -1. All our categorical features are encoded. In this paper we have classified malignant and Benign in diagnosis with 0 and

1. After encoding the dataset we have applied a neural network on these dataset and achieved accuracy.

3 Normalizer Method Normalization is a better technique to use when distribution of the data is unknown.. Data normalization is the process of rescaling one and more attributes to the range of 0 to 1. This means that the largest value for each attribute is 1 and the smallest value is 0. After applying the Label Encoder method all dataset is converted into numeric dataset. Because Label Encoder encodes all string label dataset into numeric dataset. Normalization process is known to work on numeric dataset. So after normalized data we have applied a neural network on that dataset and achieved accuracy. But again accuracy is not yet adequate. So we have applied the next process for pre-processing.

.4. Convolutional Neural Network Convolutional Neural Network is a type of neural network technique which has proven to be specifically efficient with image recognition and classification. The input is a tensor with shape (number of images) x (image width) x (image height) x (image depth) in the programming CNN. Then the image becomes abstracted to a feature map, with shape (number of images) x (feature map width) x (feature map height) x (feature map channels)after passing through a convolutional layer. The following attributes are expected in a convolutional layer within a neural network : • Width and height (hyper-parameters) defined by convolutional kernels. • The number of input channels and output channels (hyper-parameter). • The number channels (depth) of the input feature map must be equal to depth of the Convolution filter (the input channels) The convolution of input and passing its result to the next layer is done by Convolutional layers. This is similar to the response of a neuron in the visual cortex to a specific stimulus. Each and every convolutional neuron processes data only for its receptive field. It is not practical to apply this architecture to images, even though fully connected feed forward neural networks can be used to learn features as well as classify data. Due to the very large input sizes related with images, a very high number of neurons would be required, even in a simplistic architecture which is not very deep, where each pixel is a relevant variable. For example,in the second layer, a fully connected layer for an image of size 100 x 100 has 10,000 weights for each neuron. A way out to this issue is provided by the convolution operation by decreasing the number of free parameters, allowing the network to be even deeper with keeping the parameters few. Taking an example, irrespective of image size, tiling regions of size 5 x 5, each with the same shared weights, requires only 25 learnable parameters. If went by this, back propagation resolves the exploding or vanishing gradients difficulty in training traditional multi-layer neural networks with many layers. ReLU is the abbreviation of rectified linear unit, which applies the non-saturating activation functionf(x)=max(0,x). It successfully removes negative values from an activation map by setting them to zero. The nonlinear properties of the overall network and the decision function without affecting the receptive fields of the convolution layer are increased by it. Other functions are also used to extend nonlinearity, for instance the saturating hyperbolic tangent f(x)=tanh(x), f(x)=|tanh(x)| and the sigmoid function sigma(x)=(1+e^- x)^-1 . Since it trains the neural network several times faster without a large kr significant penalty to generalization accuracy, ReLU is preferred a lot more than the other functions.

5. Graphical User Interface The final part of the project includes a graphic user interface(GUI) which will act as a platform to feed fresh cell images for the module to detect whether the given image is cancerous or non cancerous.

For this we use Flask. Flask is a web application framework which is written in python. It means by using flask,with the help of the tools, libraries and technologies provided by it , a complete web application can be built. This specific web application can be anything from wiki, a web page, a blog to something as big as a commercial website or a webbased major application. Flask also supports extensions that can add application details and characteristics as if they were implemented in Flask . It has proven to be a significant tool for learning web development basics and best techniques along with the main elements of a web International Research Journal of Engineering and Technology framework that are regular to almost all frameworks. Using all these components a GUI is created which will help in the classification of a new image.

GUI 5. MODEL IMPLEMENTATION Neural Network algorithm has been applied on the dataset in this stage. Neural network here works like a human biological method. In which we have to provide the input and get the output. But in these two layers, some hidden layers are present and it becomes mandatory that some additional process must be added before calculating the final output. These added units of bias, some of additional hidden layers, calculate the activation function and the final output is generated. The following parameters for calculating and training the model have been used in this model. Fig -4: Neural Network Functionality Fig shows the basic functionality of the neural network in which after the fixed position the neurons are fired that is called threshold condition. Table -1: Parameters in CCN model Parameters used in CCN model Number of inputs 512 Number of neurons 512 Activation function Relu Number of epochs 10 6. RESULTS AND DISCUSSION In this paper we have proposed a Deep Learning with Neural Network algorithm for diagnosis and detection of breast cancer. For pre-processing breast cancer dataset , we have used the standardization method . Then we have implemented a neural network algorithm and achieved 87.64% accuracy. By using breast-histopathology-images we tested 1728 images and received 87.64% which shows promising results as compared to other machine learning algorithms. Fig -5: Result of model 7. CONCLUSIONS Cancer detection using machine learning is a system that mainly targets the early detection of cancer. With the ever increasing surge in the number of cancer diagnosis there is a need for better technology that increases the chance of survival. Hence we aim to use machine learning for early diagnosis which eventually increases the survival rate. For this, we have fed the machine with categorized data sets of malignant and benign cell images and for better results we have also shuffled these images within themselves and then have successfully trained the machine with malignant and benign data sets after which successful testing is performed with an unknown data set.

Breast cancer is one of the major causes of death in women around the world. According to the American cancer society, 41,760 women and more than 500 men died from breast cancer recently1. Breast cancer occurs in four main types: normal, benign, in-situ carcinoma and invasive carcinoma [. A benign tumor involves a minor change in the breast structure. It is not harmful and does not classify as a harmful cancer. In cases of in-situ carcinoma, the cancer is only in the mammary duct lobule system and does not affect other organs. This type is not dangerous and can be treated if diagnosed early. Invasive carcinoma is considered to be the most dangerous type of breast cancer, as it can spread to all other organs. According to the authors in [1], breast cancer can be detected using several methods including X-ray mammography, ultrasound (US), Computed Tomography (CT), Portion Emission

Tomography (PET), Magnetic Resonance Imaging (MRI) and breast temperature measurement. Usually, the golden standard is a pathological diagnosis for detecting breast cancer. This involves an image analysis of the removed tissue, which is stained in the lab to increase visibility. Hematoxylin and Eosin (H&E) are commonly used for the staining process. Breast cancer can be diagnosed using one of two approaches: histopathological image analysis or genomics. Histopathological images are microscopic images of breast tissue that are extremely useful in early treatment of the cancer. As for genomics, the authors in stated that radio1 https://www.cancer.org/ Artificial Intelligence in Medicine, Elsevier, Vol 127, May 2022 genomics is an emerging research field focusing on multi-scale associations between medical imaging and gene expression data. Radio-genomics provide both radiological and genetic features that can enhance diagnosis. It can analyze tissues at the molecular level, helping with prediction and early detection of cancer. The main difference between imaging information and radio-genomics is the critical knowledge gap between imaging at the tissue level and analyzing the underlying molecular and genetic disease biomarkers. As imaging is less precise, it may lead to over- or under-treatment. While radio-genomics is much more effective than histopathological imaging, it is rarely used because the process involves datasets that are very expensive and require high computational power. As a result, a limited number of labs conduct radio-genomics experiments [.

This research paper addresses the following research questions and highlights the deep learning models, looking at their performance, the datasets used and possibilities for breast cancer classification and detection. 1. Which deep learning models perform most effectively? We will compare deep learning models with classical machine learning models to compare their performance. We will also list the performance metrics used. 2. What are the most used features for breast cancer classification? How are these features selected and extracted? We will observe the most important features that contribute to breast cancer classification, and the methods used to extract these features. 3. What datasets are available for both gene sequencing and MRI? What feature selection and extraction methods are used? We will list and discuss all public and private datasets for gene sequencing and MRI imaging data. We will also list some of the methods used to select and extract the features. 4. Comparing gene sequence data with image data, for breast cancer detection problem, what are the drawbacks, challenges, and advantages? We will compare imaging and gene sequencing as they relate to breast cancer detection, using a tabular presentation to highlight the main differences between the two approaches. This is structured as follows:

Section 2 presents related work which includes surveys conducted in breast cancer area.

Section 3 explains the methodology used to conduct this research.

Section 4 presents the obtained results and related discussions.

Lastly, Section 5 concludes the paper and suggests future research directions. 2. Related Work Many studies have been conducted about breast cancer detection through imaging or through genomics. However, to the best of our knowledge, no research has been conducted including both techniques. The authors in [1] summarized the various techniques used to classify breast cancer using histopathological image analysis (HIA) based on different architectures of Artificial Neural Networks (ANN). The authors Artificial Intelligence in Medicine, Elsevier, Vol 127, May 2022 grouped their work according to the applied dataset. They arranged it in ascending chronological order. This work found that ANNs were first used in the field of HIA around 2012. ANNs and PNNs were the most frequently applied algorithms. However, in feature extraction, most of the work used textural and morphological features. It was clear that Deep CNNs were quite effective for early detection and diagnosis of breast cancer, leading to more successful treatment. Prediction of Non-Communicable Diseases (NCDs) was conducted using many algorithms.

In this the authors compared the performance of various classification algorithms. The classification algorithms were performed on eight NCD datasets using eight classification algorithms and a 10-fold crossvalidation method. These were evaluated using AUC as an indicator of accuracy. The authors stated that the NCD datasets have noisy data and irrelevant attributes. KNN, SVM and NN proved to be robust to this noise. In addition, they stated that the irrelevant attribute problem can be handled with some pre-processing techniques to improve the accuracy rate. Natural inspired computing (NIC) algorithms have been designed and applied to diagnose various human disorders. The authors in [3)introduced five insect-based NIC algorithms used for diagnosing diabetes and cancer. The authors found that it achieved a high level of performance in detecting different types of cancer (breast, lung, prostate and ovarian). To be more specific, breast cancer was detected using a hybridization of the guided ABC and neural networks. The authors also developed a highly effective methodology of detecting diabetes and leukemia. They concluded that the hybridization of NICs with other classification algorithms produces more precise and promising results. They mentioned that more work is required to detect different stages of diabetes and cancer.

In [4], the authors demonstrated the effectiveness of NNs in the classification of cancer diagnoses, especially in the initial stages. According to their study, the majority of NNs have shown promise in detecting tumor cells. However, the imaging approach requires high computational capacity to preprocess the images.

In [5], the authors reviewed different machine learning, deep learning and data mining algorithms related to breast cancer prediction. Several research papers on breast cancer were reviewed, with a total of 27 papers in machine learning, 4 papers in ensemble techniques and 8 papers in deep learning techniques. The authors mentioned that most of the papers used imaging, while only a few papers used genetics. The main algorithms used to predict breast cancer using genetics were SVM, decision tree and random forest. However, imaging techniques used several algorithms such as CNNs and Naïve Bayes. On the other hand, the authors

in [6] focused on gene mutation for detecting breast cancer. They mentioned that the gene prediction classification phase aims to carry out gene annotation, gene finding and gene mutation detection to ascertain the presence or absence of a cancer. They concluded that several methods can be used including regression, probability models, SVMs, NNs and deep learning. They also mentioned the many opportunities available to capture the relationship between nucleotide and feature extraction, since DNA sequencing involves a large amount of data in the form of a string sequence.

In [7], the authors examined recent studies applying deep learning to breast cancer with different imaging modalities. They organized these studies using the aspects of dataset, architecture, application and evaluation. They focused on deep learning frameworks developed in three breast imaging modalities (ultrasound, mammography and

MRI). In their work, they attempted to provide state-of-the-art findings about breast cancer imaging utilizing DLR-based CAD systems. Their study included private datasets and classification using CNNs. Artificial Intelligence in Medicine, Elsevier, Vol 127, May 2022

After studying these surveys, our contribution will involve studying genetic sequencing and imaging at the same time to predict breast cancer and to get more information that can help early diagnosis and treatment of breast cancer. We will also provide recommendations to researchers who wish to conduct research in this area. 3. Methodology Our target topic is breast cancer detection using deep learning. We ended up using around 80 of the most recent papers related to breast cancer treatment and diagnosis. Some of the papers examined only deep learning, while others used a combination of machine learning and deep learning. In our search process, we mainly used the Scopus database to obtain the articles. This is to exclude nonrefereed publications However, in Figure 1, we state the distribution of selected papers among the existing databases. The top five databases are PubMed, ScienceDirect (Elsevier), IEEE, Springer and Nature.

The imaging modalities we considered were ultrasound, radiography, mammography and magnetic resonance imaging (MRI), as well as various types of gene expression and gene sequencing. In this research, we focused on papers that implement the breast cancer detection using the techniques of AI, as well as papers that predict breast cancer using both gene data and image data. We applied the following eligibility criteria on each paper: (1) The language is English; (2) The topic is related to breast cancer detection and treatment; (3) The paper discusses hybrid models of machine learning and deep learning; (4) The paper purely discusses deep learning; (5) The paper discusses genetic expression data; (6) The paper discusses imaging data; (7) Only journal and conference publications are retained; (8) Only medical or biomedical engineering publications are kept which are related to the topic. Please note that non-refereed publications were excluded from the study. Firstly, we recorded the main information such as the name of the paper, year of publication, the list of authors and the publisher. Then, we included some information to conduct the systematic review, such as the algorithm used and whether the paper discusses only deep learning or a hybrid between DL and ML, the recorded accuracy and other performance evaluation parameters, the dataset, the features, and many other columns. We answered our research questions using these criteria. 4. Results and Discussion In this systematic study, our initial search turned up 1,000 conference and journal papers. After eliminating duplicated papers and unrelated studies that were "purely medical or about cancer in general", we ended up with 80 papers related to both ML and DL.

In machine learning method, data and output is run on the computer to create a program :

1. Sparse compact incremental learning machine (SCILM) method A new approach was designed to resolve cancer classification problem on microarray gene expression data, which take advantage of correntropy cost that makes it robust against diverse noises and outliers. Moreover, since SCILM uses l1-norm of the weights, it has sparseness, which can be applied for gene selection purposes as well. Finally, due to compact structure, the method is capable of performing classification tasks in all of the cases with only one neuron in its hidden layer. The experimental analysis in this method was performed on 26 well-known microarray data sets regarding diverse

kinds of cancers and the results showed that the strategy not only achieved significantly high accuracy but also accompanied with effectivity of each gene regarding the corresponding cancer .

2. Knowledge base system learning method A new knowledge-based system for classification of cancer disease was proposed using clustering, noise removal, and classification techniques. Expectation Maximization (EM) was used as a clustering method to cluster the data in similar groups. Classification and Regression Trees (CART) were used to generate the fuzzy rules to be used for the classification of cancer disease in the knowledge-based system of fuzzy rule-based reasoning method. To overcome the multicollinearity issue, Principal Component Analysis (PCA) was incorporated in the current knowledge-based system. Experimental results on Wisconsin Diagnostic Breast Cancer and Mammographic mass datasets showed that current approach remarkably improves the prediction accuracy of breast cancer. The knowledge-based system can be used .

3. Gauss-Newton representation based learning method A novel Gauss-Newton representation based algorithm (GNRBA) for breast cancer classification. It uses the sparse representation with training sample selection. Until now, sparse representation has been successfully applied in pattern recognition only. This method introduces a novel Gauss-Newton based approach to find the optimal weights for the training samples for classification. In addition, it evaluates the sparsity in a computationally efficient way as compared to the conventional l1-norm method. The effectiveness of the GNRBA is examined on the Wisconsin Breast Cancer Database (WBCD) and the Wisconsin Diagnosis Breast Cancer (WDBC) database from the UCI Machine Learning repository. Various performance measures like classification accuracy, sensitivity, specificity, confusion matrices, a statistical test and the area under the receiver operating characteristic (AUC) are reported to show the superiority of the proposed method as compared to classical models [17].

4. Gene expression learning method Studying the characteristics of thousands of genes simultaneously offered a deep insight into cancer classification problem. It introduced an abundant amount of data ready to be explored. It has also been applied in a wide range of applications such as drug discovery, cancer prediction and diagnosis which is a very important issue for cancer treatment . Besides, it helps in understanding the function of genes and the interaction between genes in

normal and abnormal conditions . That is done by monitoring the behavior of genes, gene expression data under different conditions. Ensemble classifiers increase not only the performance of the classification, but also the confidence of the results. The motivations beyond using ensemble classifiers are that the results are less dependent on peculiarities of a single training set and because the ensemble system outperforms the performance of the best base classifier in the ensemble [19].

5. Ensemble predictive modeling framework learning method Molecular changes often precede clinical presentation of diseases and can be useful surrogates with potential to assist in informed clinical decision making. Recent studies have demonstrated the usefulness of modeling approaches such as classification that can predict the clinical outcomes from molecular expression profiles. While useful, a majority of these approaches implicitly use all molecular markers as features in the classification process often resulting in sparse high-dimensional projection of

the samples often comparable to that of the sample size. Ensemble classification approach is used for predicting good and poorprognosis breast cancer samples from their molecular expression profiles [20]. In contrast to traditional single and ensemble classifiers, the proposed approach uses multiple base classifiers with varying feature sets obtained from two-dimensional projection of the samples in conjunction with a majority voting strategy for predicting the class labels .

In contrast to earlier implementation, base classifiers in the ensembles are chosen based on maximal sensitivity and minimal redundancy by choosing only those with low average cosine distance. The resulting ensemble sets are subsequently modeled as undirected graphs. Performance of four different classification algorithms is shown to be better within the proposed ensemble framework in contrast to using them as traditional single classifier systems. Design of an efficient ensemble predictive modeling classification framework for prediction of breast density class .

6. Convolution neural network learning method Deep convolutional neural networks (CNNs) were designed to obtain more discriminative description of cancer tissues. Benefiting from the discriminative representation, metric learning layers are proposed to further improve performance of the deep structure. The bestperforming model restricts the depth of back I J Mutil Re App St Volume 1 Issue 1, 2017 PP. 1-8 6|Page propagation of joint training in only the metric learning layers. Relation between metric learning layers and tradition CNNs structures seems like parasitism relationship between species, where one species, the parasite, benefits at the expense of the other . Therefore, the method is named as parasitic metric learning net. To confirm veracity of this method, classification experiments on breast mass images of two widely used databases were performed . Comparing performance of the current method with traditional ones, competitive results were achieved. Meanwhile, the parameter updating strategy for parasitic metric net may inspire a way of improving performance of a pre-trained CNNs model on particular medical image processing or other computer vision tasks . Training pipeline of the proposed parasitic metric learning net .We discussed the concepts of machine learning while we outlined their application in cancer prediction/prognosis. Most of the studies that have been proposed the last years and focus on the development of predictive models using supervised machine learning methods and classification algorithms aiming to predict valid disease outcomes. Based on the analysis of their results, it is evident that the integration of multidimensional heterogeneous data, combined with the application of different techniques for feature selection and classification can provide promising tools for inference in the cancer domain.

EXPERIMENT AND METHODOLOGY :.

1 Data-sets A malignant tumour that has developed from cells of the breast is breast cancer. Although some of the scientifically known risk factors (i.e. ageing, genetic risk factors, family history, menstrual periods, not having children, obesity) that increase a woman's chance of developing breast cancer, the exact causes or some of these risk factors that causes cells to become cancerous are not exactly known by them. Research is under way to learn more and scientists are making great progress in understanding how certain changes in DNA can cause normal breast cells to become cancerous. This part of the project includes the research about the available dataset that can be used for the project. The initial dataset that we planned on working had certain drawbacks. CBIS-DDSM dataset: Neither the

analytics nor the experimental validation of the data were sufficient to move forward with the project. There was no exact data regarding the classification of tumours into benign and malignant in case of scan images of patients. One the most important demerit of this dataset was the improper organization of data and huge redundant records which can cause glitches in the training process. Hence it was concluded that evaluation based on detection rate and accuracy levels with this data-set is not appropriate. Breast cancer Wisconsin data-set: This dataset was a text type data-set which had a classified set of data into malignant and benign tumours based on the cell features threshold values for various features like cell radius, perimeter, area, symmetry and other such International Research Journal of Engineering and Technology . We didn't go for this data-set since we planned on a better version of cancer detection model which focused on images

2 Pre-processing data Data preprocessing is a data mining technique that is used for filter data in a usable format. Because the real-world data-set is almost available in different formats. It's not available as per our requirement so it must fit the data-set in an understandable format. Data pre processing is a proven method of resolving such issues. Data pre-processing converts the data-set into usable format for pre-processing. We have used a standardization method to pre- process the data-set. Encoder Method: Label Encoder is an efficient tool for encoding the levels of the categorical features into numeric values. Label Encoder encode labels with value between 0 and classes -1. All our categorical features are encoded. In this paper we have classified malignant and Benign in diagnosis with 0 and 1. After encoding the dataset we have applied a neural network on these dataset and achieved accuracy.

3 Normalizer Method Normalization is a better technique to use when distribution of the data is unknown.. Data normalization is the process of rescaling one and more attributes to the range of 0 to 1. This means that the largest value for each attribute is 1 and the smallest value is 0. After applying the Label Encoder method all dataset is converted into numeric dataset. Because Label Encoder encodes all string label dataset into numeric dataset. Normalization process is known to work on numeric dataset. So after normalized data we have applied a neural network on that dataset and achieved accuracy. But again accuracy is not yet adequate. So we have applied the next process for pre-processing.

.4. Convolutional Neural Network Convolutional Neural Network is a type of neural network technique which has proven to be specifically efficient with image recognition and classification. The input is a tensor with shape (number of images) x (image width) x (image height) x (image depth) in the programming CNN. Then the image becomes abstracted to a feature map, with shape (number of images) x (feature map width) x (feature map height) x (feature map channels)after passing through a convolutional layer. The following attributes are expected in a convolutional layer within a neural network : • Width and height (hyper-parameters) defined by convolutional kernels. • The number of input channels and output channels (hyper-parameter). • The number channels (depth) of the input feature map must be equal to depth of the Convolution filter (the input channels) The convolution of input and passing its result to the next layer is done by Convolutional layers. This is similar to the response of a neuron in the visual cortex to a specific stimulus. Each and every convolutional neuron processes data only for its receptive field. It is not practical to apply this architecture to images, even though fully connected feed forward neural networks can be used to learn features as well as classify data. Due to the very large input sizes related with images, a very high number of neurons would be required, even in a simplistic architecture which is not very deep, where each pixel is a relevant variable. For example,in the second layer, a fully connected layer for an image of size 100 x 100 has 10,000 weights for each neuron. A way out to this issue is provided by the convolution operation by decreasing the number of free parameters, allowing the network to be even deeper with keeping the parameters few. Taking an example, irrespective of image size, tiling regions of size 5 x 5, each with the same shared weights, requires only 25 learnable parameters. If went by this, back propagation resolves the exploding or vanishing gradients difficulty in training traditional multi-layer neural networks with many layers. ReLU is the abbreviation of rectified linear unit, which applies the non-saturating activation functionf(x)=max(0,x). It successfully removes negative values from an activation map by setting them to zero. The nonlinear properties of the overall network and the decision function without affecting the receptive fields of the convolution layer are increased by it. Other functions are also used to extend nonlinearity, for instance the saturating hyperbolic tangent f(x)=tanh(x), f(x)=|tanh(x)| and the sigmoid function sigma(x)=(1+e^- x)^-1 . Since it trains the neural network several times faster without a large kr significant penalty to generalization accuracy, ReLU is preferred a lot more than the other functions.

5. Graphical User Interface The final part of the project includes a graphic user interface(GUI) which will act as a platform to feed fresh cell images for the module to detect whether the given image is cancerous or non cancerous. For this we use Flask. Flask is a web application framework which is written in python. It means by using flask,with the help of the tools, libraries and technologies provided by it , a complete web application can be built. This specific web application can be anything from wiki, a web page, a blog to something as big as a commercial website or a webbased major application. Flask also supports extensions that can add application details and characteristics as if they were implemented in Flask . It has proven to be a significant tool for learning web development basics and best techniques along with the main elements of a web International Research Journal of Engineering and Technology framework that are regular to almost all frameworks. Using all these components a GUI is created which will help in the classification of a new image.

GUI 5. MODEL IMPLEMENTATION Neural Network algorithm has been applied on the dataset in this stage. Neural network here works like a human biological method. In which we have to provide the input and get the output. But in these two layers, some hidden layers are present and it becomes mandatory that some additional process must be added before calculating the final output. These added units of bias, some of additional hidden layers, calculate the activation function and the final output is generated. The following parameters for calculating and training the model have been used in this model. Fig -4: Neural Network Functionality Fig shows the basic functionality of the neural network in which after the fixed position the neurons are fired that is called threshold condition. Table -1: Parameters in CCN model Parameters used in CCN model Number of inputs 512 Number of neurons 512 Activation function Relu Number of epochs 10 6. RESULTS AND DISCUSSION In this paper we have proposed a Deep Learning with Neural Network algorithm for diagnosis and detection of breast cancer. For pre-processing breast cancer dataset , we have used the standardization method . Then we have implemented a neural network algorithm and achieved

87.64% accuracy. By using breast-histopathology-images we tested 1728 images and received 87.64% which shows promising results as compared to other machine learning algorithms. Fig -5: Result of model 7. CONCLUSIONS Cancer detection using machine learning is a system that mainly targets the early detection of cancer. With the ever increasing surge in the number of cancer diagnosis there is a need for better technology that increases the chance of survival. Hence we aim to use machine learning for early diagnosis which eventually increases the survival rate. For this, we have fed the machine with categorized data sets of malignant and benign cell images and for better results we have also shuffled these images within themselves and then have successfully trained the machine with malignant and benign data sets after which successful testing is performed with an unknown data set.

Breast cancer is one of the major causes of death in women around the world. According to the American cancer society, 41,760 women and more than 500 men died from breast cancer recently1. Breast cancer occurs in four main types: normal, benign, in-situ carcinoma and invasive carcinoma [. A benign tumor involves a minor change in the breast structure. It is not harmful and does not classify as a harmful cancer. In cases of in-situ carcinoma, the cancer is only in the mammary duct lobule system and does not affect other organs. This type is not dangerous and can be treated if diagnosed early. Invasive carcinoma is considered to be the most dangerous type of breast cancer, as it can spread to all other organs. According to the authors in [1], breast cancer can be detected using several methods including X-ray mammography, ultrasound (US), Computed Tomography (CT), Portion Emission Tomography (PET), Magnetic Resonance Imaging (MRI) and breast temperature measurement. Usually, the golden standard is a pathological diagnosis for detecting breast cancer. This involves an image analysis of the removed tissue, which is stained in the lab to increase visibility. Hematoxylin and Eosin (H&E) are commonly used for the staining process. Breast cancer can be diagnosed using one of two approaches: histopathological image analysis or genomics. Histopathological images are microscopic images of breast tissue that are extremely useful in early treatment of the cancer. As for genomics, the authors in stated that radio1 https://www.cancer.org/ Artificial Intelligence in Medicine, Elsevier, Vol 127, May 2022 genomics is an emerging research field focusing on multi-scale associations between medical imaging and gene expression data. Radio-genomics provide both radiological and genetic features that can enhance diagnosis. It can analyze tissues at the molecular level, helping with prediction and early detection of cancer. The main difference between imaging information and radio-genomics is the critical knowledge gap between imaging at the tissue level and analyzing the underlying molecular and genetic disease biomarkers. As imaging is less precise, it may lead to over- or under-treatment. While radio-genomics is much more effective than histopathological imaging, it is rarely used because the process involves datasets that are very expensive and require high computational power. As a result, a limited number of labs conduct radio-genomics experiments [.

This research paper addresses the following research questions and highlights the deep learning models, looking at their performance, the datasets used and possibilities for breast cancer classification and detection. 1. Which deep learning models perform most effectively? We will compare deep learning models with classical machine learning models to compare their performance. We will also list the performance metrics used. 2. What are the most used features for breast cancer classification? How are these features selected and extracted? We will observe the most important features that contribute to breast cancer classification, and the methods used to extract these features. 3. What datasets are available for both gene sequencing and MRI? What feature selection and extraction methods are used? We will list and discuss all public and private datasets for gene sequencing and MRI imaging data. We will also list some of the methods used to select and extract the features. 4. Comparing gene sequence data with image data, for breast cancer detection problem, what are the drawbacks, challenges, and advantages? We will compare imaging and gene sequencing as they relate to breast cancer detection, using a tabular presentation to highlight the main differences between the two approaches. This is structured as follows:

Section 2 presents related work which includes surveys conducted in breast cancer area.

Section 3 explains the methodology used to conduct this research.

Section 4 presents the obtained results and related discussions.

Lastly, Section 5 concludes the paper and suggests future research directions. 2. Related Work Many studies have been conducted about breast cancer detection through imaging or through genomics. However, to the best of our knowledge, no research has been conducted including both techniques. The authors in [1] summarized the various techniques used to classify breast cancer using histopathological image analysis (HIA) based on different architectures of Artificial Neural Networks (ANN). The authors Artificial Intelligence in Medicine, Elsevier, Vol 127, May 2022 grouped their work according to the applied dataset. They arranged it in ascending chronological order. This work found that ANNs were first used in the field of HIA around 2012. ANNs and PNNs were the most frequently applied algorithms. However, in feature extraction, most of the work used textural and morphological features. It was clear that Deep CNNs were quite effective for early detection and diagnosis of breast cancer, leading to more successful treatment. Prediction of Non-Communicable Diseases (NCDs) was conducted using many algorithms.

In this the authors compared the performance of various classification algorithms. The classification algorithms were performed on eight NCD datasets using eight classification algorithms and a 10-fold crossvalidation method. These were evaluated using AUC as an indicator of accuracy. The authors stated that the NCD datasets have noisy data and irrelevant attributes. KNN, SVM and NN proved to be robust to this noise. In addition, they stated that the irrelevant attribute problem can be handled with some pre-processing techniques to improve the accuracy rate. Natural inspired computing (NIC) algorithms have been designed and applied to diagnose various human disorders. The authors in [3)introduced five insect-based NIC algorithms used for diagnosing diabetes and cancer. The authors found that it achieved a high level of performance in detecting different types of cancer (breast, lung, prostate and ovarian). To be more specific, breast cancer was detected using a hybridization of the guided ABC and neural networks. The authors also developed a highly effective methodology of detecting diabetes and leukemia. They concluded that the hybridization of NICs with other classification algorithms produces more precise and promising results. They mentioned that more work is required to detect different stages of diabetes and cancer.

In [4], the authors demonstrated the effectiveness of NNs in the classification of cancer diagnoses, especially in the initial stages. According to their study, the majority of NNs have shown promise in detecting tumor cells.

However, the imaging approach requires high computational capacity to preprocess the images.

In [5], the authors reviewed different machine learning, deep learning and data mining algorithms related to breast cancer prediction. Several research papers on breast cancer were reviewed, with a total of 27 papers in machine learning, 4 papers in ensemble techniques and 8 papers in deep learning techniques. The authors mentioned that most of the papers used imaging, while only a few papers used genetics. The main algorithms used to predict breast cancer using genetics were SVM, decision tree and random forest. However, imaging techniques used several algorithms such as CNNs and Naïve Bayes. On the other hand, the authors

in [6] focused on gene mutation for detecting breast cancer. They mentioned that the gene prediction classification phase aims to carry out gene annotation, gene finding and gene mutation detection to ascertain the presence or absence of a cancer. They concluded that several methods can be used including regression, probability models, SVMs, NNs and deep learning. They also mentioned the many opportunities available to capture the relationship between nucleotide and feature extraction, since DNA sequencing involves a large amount of data in the form of a string sequence.

In [7], the authors examined recent studies applying deep learning to breast cancer with different imaging modalities. They organized these studies using the aspects of dataset, architecture, application and evaluation. They focused on deep learning frameworks developed in three breast imaging modalities (ultrasound, mammography and MRI). In their work, they attempted to provide state-of-the-art findings about breast cancer imaging utilizing DLR-based CAD systems. Their study included private datasets and classification using CNNs. Artificial Intelligence in Medicine, Elsevier, Vol 127, May 2022

After studying these surveys, our contribution will involve studying genetic sequencing and imaging at the same time to predict breast cancer and to get more information that can help early diagnosis and treatment of breast cancer. We will also provide recommendations to researchers who wish to conduct research in this area. 3. Methodology Our target topic is breast cancer detection using deep learning. We ended up using around 80 of the most recent papers related to breast cancer treatment and diagnosis. Some of the papers examined only deep learning, while others used a combination of machine learning and deep learning. In our search process, we mainly used the Scopus database to obtain the articles. This is to exclude nonrefereed publications However, in Figure 1, we state the distribution of selected papers among the existing databases. The top five databases are PubMed, ScienceDirect (Elsevier), IEEE, Springer and Nature.

The imaging modalities we considered were ultrasound, radiography, mammography and magnetic resonance imaging (MRI), as well as various types of gene expression and gene sequencing. In this research, we focused on papers that implement the breast cancer detection using the techniques of AI, as well as papers that predict breast cancer using both gene data and image data. We applied the following eligibility criteria on each paper: (1) The language is English; (2) The topic is related to breast cancer detection and treatment; (3) The paper discusses hybrid models of machine learning and deep learning; (4) The paper purely discusses deep learning; (5) The paper discusses genetic expression data; (6) The paper discusses imaging data; (7) Only journal and conference publications are retained; (8) Only medical or biomedical engineering publications are kept which are related to the topic. Please note that non-refereed publications were excluded from the study. Firstly, we recorded the main information such as the name of the paper, year of publication, the list of authors and the publisher. Then, we included some information to conduct the systematic review, such as the algorithm used and whether the paper discusses only deep learning or a hybrid between DL and ML, the recorded accuracy and other performance evaluation parameters, the dataset, the features, and many other columns. We answered our research questions using these criteria. 4. Results and Discussion In this systematic study, our initial search turned up 1,000 conference and journal papers. After eliminating duplicated papers and unrelated studies that were "purely medical or about cancer in general", we ended up with 80 papers related to both ML and DL.

In machine learning method, data and output is run on the computer to create a program :

1. Sparse compact incremental learning machine (SCILM) method A new approach was designed to resolve cancer classification problem on microarray gene expression data, which take advantage of correntropy cost that makes it robust against diverse noises and outliers. Moreover, since SCILM uses l1-norm of the weights, it has sparseness, which can be applied for gene selection purposes as well. Finally, due to compact structure, the method is capable of performing classification tasks in all of the cases with only one neuron in its hidden layer. The experimental analysis in this method was performed on 26 well-known microarray data sets regarding diverse kinds of cancers and the results showed that the strategy not only achieved significantly high accuracy but also accompanied with effectivity of each gene regarding the corresponding cancer .

2. Knowledge base system learning method A new knowledge-based system for classification of cancer disease was proposed using clustering, noise removal, and classification techniques. Expectation Maximization (EM) was used as a clustering method to cluster the data in similar groups. Classification and Regression Trees (CART) were used to generate the fuzzy rules to be used for the classification of cancer disease in the knowledge-based system of fuzzy rule-based reasoning method. To overcome the multicollinearity issue, Principal Component Analysis (PCA) was incorporated in the current knowledge-based system. Experimental results on Wisconsin Diagnostic Breast Cancer and Mammographic mass datasets showed that current approach remarkably improves the prediction accuracy of breast cancer. The knowledge-based system can be used .

3. Gauss-Newton representation based learning method A novel Gauss-Newton representation based algorithm (GNRBA) for breast cancer classification. It uses the sparse representation with training sample selection. Until now, sparse representation has been successfully applied in pattern recognition only. This method introduces a novel Gauss-Newton based approach to find the optimal weights for the training samples for classification. In addition, it evaluates the sparsity in a computationally efficient way as compared to the conventional l1-norm method. The effectiveness of the GNRBA is examined on the Wisconsin Breast Cancer Database (WBCD) and the Wisconsin Diagnosis Breast Cancer (WDBC) database from the UCI Machine Learning repository. Various performance measures like classification accuracy, sensitivity, specificity, confusion matrices, a statistical test and the area under the receiver operating characteristic (AUC) are reported to show the superiority of the proposed

method as compared to classical models [17].

4. Gene expression learning method Studying the characteristics of thousands of genes simultaneously offered a deep insight into cancer classification problem. It introduced an abundant amount of data ready to be explored. It has also been applied in a wide range of applications such as drug discovery, cancer prediction and diagnosis which is a very important issue for cancer treatment . Besides, it helps in understanding the function of genes and the interaction between genes in

normal and abnormal conditions . That is done by monitoring the behavior of genes, gene expression data under different conditions. Ensemble classifiers increase not only the performance of the classification, but also the confidence of the results. The motivations beyond using ensemble classifiers are that the results are less dependent on peculiarities of a single training set and because the ensemble system outperforms the performance of the best base classifier in the ensemble [19].

5. Ensemble predictive modeling framework learning method Molecular changes often precede clinical presentation of diseases and can be useful surrogates with potential to assist in informed clinical decision making. Recent studies have demonstrated the usefulness of modeling approaches such as classification that can predict the clinical outcomes from molecular expression profiles. While useful, a majority of these approaches implicitly use all molecular markers as features in the classification process often resulting in sparse high-dimensional projection of the samples often comparable to that of the sample size. Ensemble classification approach is used for predicting good and poorprognosis breast cancer samples from their molecular expression profiles [20]. In contrast to traditional single and ensemble classifiers, the proposed approach uses multiple base classifiers with varying feature sets obtained from two-dimensional projection of the samples in conjunction with a majority voting strategy for predicting the class labels .

In contrast to earlier implementation, base classifiers in the ensembles are chosen based on maximal sensitivity and minimal redundancy by choosing only those with low average cosine distance. The resulting ensemble sets are subsequently modeled as undirected graphs. Performance of four different classification algorithms is shown to be better within the proposed ensemble framework in contrast to using them as traditional single classifier systems. Design of an efficient ensemble predictive modeling classification framework for prediction of breast density class .

6. Convolution neural network learning method Deep convolutional neural networks (CNNs) were designed to obtain more discriminative description of cancer tissues. Benefiting from the discriminative representation, metric learning layers are proposed to further improve performance of the deep structure. The bestperforming model restricts the depth of back I J Mutil Re App St Volume 1 Issue 1, 2017 PP. 1-8 6|Page propagation of joint training in only the metric learning layers. Relation between metric learning layers and tradition CNNs structures seems like parasitism relationship between species, where one species, the parasite, benefits at the expense of the other . Therefore, the method is named as parasitic metric learning net. To confirm veracity of this method, classification experiments on breast mass images of two widely used databases were performed . Comparing performance of the current method with traditional ones, competitive results were achieved. Meanwhile, the parameter updating

strategy for parasitic metric net may inspire a way of improving performance of a pre-trained CNNs model on particular medical image processing or other computer vision tasks . Training pipeline of the proposed parasitic metric learning net .We discussed the concepts of machine learning while we outlined their application in cancer prediction/prognosis. Most of the studies that have been proposed the last years and focus on the development of predictive models using supervised machine learning methods and classification algorithms aiming to predict valid disease outcomes. Based on the analysis of their results, it is evident that the integration of multidimensional heterogeneous data, combined with the application of different techniques for feature selection and classification can provide promising tools for inference in the cancer domain.

EXPERIMENT AND METHODOLOGY :.

1 Data-sets A malignant tumour that has developed from cells of the breast is breast cancer. Although some of the scientifically known risk factors (i.e. ageing, genetic risk factors, family history, menstrual periods, not having children, obesity) that increase a woman's chance of developing breast cancer, the exact causes or some of these risk factors that causes cells to become cancerous are not exactly known by them. Research is under way to learn more and scientists are making great progress in understanding how certain changes in DNA can cause normal breast cells to become cancerous. This part of the project includes the research about the available dataset that can be used for the project. The initial dataset that we planned on working had certain drawbacks. CBIS-DDSM dataset: Neither the analytics nor the experimental validation of the data were sufficient to move forward with the project. There was no exact data regarding the classification of tumours into benign and malignant in case of scan images of patients. One the most important demerit of this dataset was the improper organization of data and huge redundant records which can cause glitches in the training process. Hence it was concluded that evaluation based on detection rate and accuracy levels with this data-set is not appropriate. Breast cancer Wisconsin data-set: This dataset was a text type data-set which had a classified set of data into malignant and benign tumours based on the cell features threshold values for various features like cell radius, perimeter, area, symmetry and other such International Research Journal of Engineering and Technology . We didn't go for this data-set since we planned on a better version of cancer detection model which focused on images

2 Pre-processing data Data preprocessing is a data mining technique that is used for filter data in a usable format. Because the real-world data-set is almost available in different formats. It's not available as per our requirement so it must fit the data-set in an understandable format. Data pre processing is a proven method of resolving such issues. Data pre-processing converts the data-set into usable format for pre-processing. We have used a standardization method to pre- process the data-set. Encoder Method: Label Encoder is an efficient tool for encoding the levels of the categorical features into numeric values. Label Encoder encode labels with value between 0 and classes -1. All our categorical features are encoded. In this paper we have classified malignant and Benign in diagnosis with 0 and 1. After encoding the dataset we have applied a neural network on these dataset and achieved accuracy.

3 Normalizer Method Normalization is a better technique to use when distribution of the data is unknown.. Data normalization is the process of rescaling one and more attributes to the range of 0 to 1. This means that the

largest value for each attribute is 1 and the smallest value is 0. After applying the Label Encoder method all dataset is converted into numeric dataset. Because Label Encoder encodes all string label dataset into numeric dataset. Normalization process is known to work on numeric dataset. So after normalized data we have applied a neural network on that dataset and achieved accuracy. But again accuracy is not yet adequate. So we have applied the next process for pre-processing.

.4. Convolutional Neural Network Convolutional Neural Network is a type of neural network technique which has proven to be specifically efficient with image recognition and classification. The input is a tensor with shape (number of images) x (image width) x (image height) x (image depth) in the programming CNN. Then the image becomes abstracted to a feature map, with shape (number of images) x (feature map width) x (feature map height) x (feature map channels)after passing through a convolutional layer. The following attributes are expected in a convolutional layer within a neural network : • Width and height (hyper-parameters) defined by convolutional kernels. • The number of input channels and output channels (hyper-parameter). • The number channels (depth) of the input feature map must be equal to depth of the Convolution filter (the input channels) The convolution of input and passing its result to the next layer is done by Convolutional layers. This is similar to the response of a neuron in the visual cortex to a specific stimulus. Each and every convolutional neuron processes data only for its receptive field. It is not practical to apply this architecture to images, even though fully connected feed forward neural networks can be used to learn features as well as classify data. Due to the very large input sizes related with images, a very high number of neurons would be required, even in a simplistic architecture which is not very deep, where each pixel is a relevant variable. For example,in the second layer, a fully connected layer for an image of size 100 x 100 has 10,000 weights for each neuron. A way out to this issue is provided by the convolution operation by decreasing the number of free parameters, allowing the network to be even deeper with keeping the parameters few. Taking an example, irrespective of image size, tiling regions of size 5 x 5, each with the same shared weights, requires only 25 learnable parameters. If went by this, back propagation resolves the exploding or vanishing gradients difficulty in training traditional multi-layer neural networks with many layers. ReLU is the abbreviation of rectified linear unit, which applies the non-saturating activation functionf(x)=max(0,x). It successfully removes negative values from an activation map by setting them to zero. The nonlinear properties of the overall network and the decision function without affecting the receptive fields of the convolution layer are increased by it. Other functions are also used to extend nonlinearity, for instance the saturating hyperbolic tangent f(x)=tanh(x), f(x)=|tanh(x)| and the sigmoid function sigma(x)=(1+e^- x)^-1 . Since it trains the neural network several times faster without a large kr significant penalty to generalization accuracy, ReLU is preferred a lot more than the other functions.

5. Graphical User Interface The final part of the project includes a graphic user interface(GUI) which will act as a platform to feed fresh cell images for the module to detect whether the given image is cancerous or non cancerous. For this we use Flask. Flask is a web application framework which is written in python. It means by using flask,with the help of the tools, libraries and technologies provided by it , a complete web application can be built. This specific web application can be anything from wiki, a web page, a blog to something as big as a commercial website or a

webbased major application. Flask also supports extensions that can add application details and characteristics as if they were implemented in Flask . It has proven to be a significant tool for learning web development basics and best techniques along with the main elements of a web International Research Journal of Engineering and Technology framework that are regular to almost all frameworks. Using all these components a GUI is created which will help in the classification of a new image.

GUI 5. MODEL IMPLEMENTATION Neural Network algorithm has been applied on the dataset in this stage. Neural network here works like a human biological method. In which we have to provide the input and get the output. But in these two layers, some hidden layers are present and it becomes mandatory that some additional process must be added before calculating the final output. These added units of bias, some of additional hidden layers, calculate the activation function and the final output is generated. The following parameters for calculating and training the model have been used in this model. Fig -4: Neural Network Functionality Fig shows the basic functionality of the neural network in which after the fixed position the neurons are fired that is called threshold condition. Table -1: Parameters in CCN model Parameters used in CCN model Number of inputs 512 Number of neurons 512 Activation function Relu Number of epochs 10 6. RESULTS AND DISCUSSION In this paper we have proposed a Deep Learning with Neural Network algorithm for diagnosis and detection of breast cancer. For pre-processing breast cancer dataset , we have used the standardization method . Then we have implemented a neural network algorithm and achieved 87.64% accuracy. By using breast-histopathology-images we tested 1728 images and received 87.64% which shows promising results as compared to other machine learning algorithms. Fig -5: Result of model 7. CONCLUSIONS Cancer detection using machine learning is a system that mainly targets the early detection of cancer. With the ever increasing surge in the number of cancer diagnosis there is a need for better technology that increases the chance of survival. Hence we aim to use machine learning for early diagnosis which eventually increases the survival rate. For this, we have fed the machine with categorized data sets of malignant and benign cell images and for better results we have also shuffled these images within themselves and then have successfully trained the machine with malignant and benign data sets after which successful testing is performed with an unknown data set.

Breast cancer is one of the major causes of death in women around the world. According to the American cancer society, 41,760 women and more than 500 men died from breast cancer recently1. Breast cancer occurs in four main types: normal, benign, in-situ carcinoma and invasive carcinoma [. A benign tumor involves a minor change in the breast structure. It is not harmful and does not classify as a harmful cancer. In cases of in-situ carcinoma, the cancer is only in the mammary duct lobule system and does not affect other organs. This type is not dangerous and can be treated if diagnosed early. Invasive carcinoma is considered to be the most dangerous type of breast cancer, as it can spread to all other organs. According to the authors in [1], breast cancer can be detected using several methods including X-ray mammography, ultrasound (US), Computed Tomography (CT), Portion Emission Tomography (PET), Magnetic Resonance Imaging (MRI) and breast temperature measurement. Usually, the golden standard is a pathological diagnosis for detecting breast cancer. This involves an image analysis of the removed tissue, which is stained in the lab to increase visibility. Hematoxylin and Eosin (H&E) are commonly used for the staining process. Breast cancer can be diagnosed using one of two approaches: histopathological image analysis or genomics. Histopathological images are microscopic images of breast tissue that are extremely useful in early treatment of the cancer. As for genomics, the authors in stated that radio1 https://www.cancer.org/ Artificial Intelligence in Medicine, Elsevier, Vol 127, May 2022 genomics is an emerging research field focusing on multi-scale associations between medical imaging and gene expression data. Radio-genomics provide both radiological and genetic features that can enhance diagnosis. It can analyze tissues at the molecular level, helping with prediction and early detection of cancer. The main difference between imaging information and radio-genomics is the critical knowledge gap between imaging at the tissue level and analyzing the underlying molecular and genetic disease biomarkers. As imaging is less precise, it may lead to over- or under-treatment. While radio-genomics is much more effective than histopathological imaging, it is rarely used because the process involves datasets that are very expensive and require high computational power. As a result, a limited number of labs conduct radio-genomics experiments [.

This research paper addresses the following research questions and highlights the deep learning models, looking at their performance, the datasets used and possibilities for breast cancer classification and detection. 1. Which deep learning models perform most effectively? We will compare deep learning models with classical machine learning models to compare their performance. We will also list the performance metrics used. 2. What are the most used features for breast cancer classification? How are these features selected and extracted? We will observe the most important features that contribute to breast cancer classification, and the methods used to extract these features. 3. What datasets are available for both gene sequencing and MRI? What feature selection and extraction methods are used? We will list and discuss all public and private datasets for gene sequencing and MRI imaging data. We will also list some of the methods used to select and extract the features. 4. Comparing gene sequence data with image data, for breast cancer detection problem, what are the drawbacks, challenges, and advantages? We will compare imaging and gene sequencing as they relate to breast cancer detection, using a tabular presentation to highlight the main differences between the two approaches. This is structured as follows:

Section 2 presents related work which includes surveys conducted in breast cancer area.

Section 3 explains the methodology used to conduct this research.

Section 4 presents the obtained results and related discussions.

Lastly, Section 5 concludes the paper and suggests future research directions. 2. Related Work Many studies have been conducted about breast cancer detection through imaging or through genomics. However, to the best of our knowledge, no research has been conducted including both techniques. The authors in [1] summarized the various techniques used to classify breast cancer using histopathological image analysis (HIA) based on different architectures of Artificial Neural Networks (ANN). The authors Artificial Intelligence in Medicine, Elsevier, Vol 127, May 2022 grouped their work according to the applied dataset. They arranged it in ascending chronological order. This work found that ANNs were first used in the field of HIA around 2012. ANNs and PNNs were the most frequently applied algorithms. However, in feature extraction, most of the work used textural and morphological features. It was clear that Deep CNNs were quite effective for early detection and diagnosis of breast cancer, leading to more successful treatment. Prediction of Non-Communicable Diseases (NCDs) was conducted using many algorithms.

In this the authors compared the performance of various classification algorithms. The classification algorithms were performed on eight NCD datasets using eight classification algorithms and a 10-fold crossvalidation method. These were evaluated using AUC as an indicator of accuracy. The authors stated that the NCD datasets have noisy data and irrelevant attributes. KNN, SVM and NN proved to be robust to this noise. In addition, they stated that the irrelevant attribute problem can be handled with some pre-processing techniques to improve the accuracy rate. Natural inspired computing (NIC) algorithms have been designed and applied to diagnose various human disorders. The authors in [3)introduced five insect-based NIC algorithms used for diagnosing diabetes and cancer. The authors found that it achieved a high level of performance in detecting different types of cancer (breast, lung, prostate and ovarian). To be more specific, breast cancer was detected using a hybridization of the guided ABC and neural networks. The authors also developed a highly effective methodology of detecting diabetes and leukemia. They concluded that the hybridization of NICs with other classification algorithms produces more precise and promising results. They mentioned that more work is required to detect different stages of diabetes and cancer.

In [4], the authors demonstrated the effectiveness of NNs in the classification of cancer diagnoses, especially in the initial stages. According to their study, the majority of NNs have shown promise in detecting tumor cells. However, the imaging approach requires high computational capacity to preprocess the images.

In [5], the authors reviewed different machine learning, deep learning and data mining algorithms related to breast cancer prediction. Several research papers on breast cancer were reviewed, with a total of 27 papers in machine learning, 4 papers in ensemble techniques and 8 papers in deep learning techniques. The authors mentioned that most of the papers used imaging, while only a few papers used genetics. The main algorithms used to predict breast cancer using genetics were SVM, decision tree and random forest. However, imaging techniques used several algorithms such as CNNs and Naïve Bayes. On the other hand, the authors

in [6] focused on gene mutation for detecting breast cancer. They mentioned that the gene prediction classification phase aims to carry out gene annotation, gene finding and gene mutation detection to ascertain the presence or absence of a cancer. They concluded that several methods can be used including regression, probability models, SVMs, NNs and deep learning. They also mentioned the many opportunities available to capture the relationship between nucleotide and feature extraction, since DNA sequencing involves a large amount of data in the form of a string sequence.

In [7], the authors examined recent studies applying deep learning to breast cancer with different imaging modalities. They organized these studies using the aspects of dataset, architecture, application and evaluation. They focused on deep learning frameworks developed in three breast imaging modalities (ultrasound, mammography and MRI). In their work, they attempted to provide state-of-the-art findings about breast cancer imaging utilizing DLR-based CAD systems. Their study included private datasets and classification using CNNs. Artificial Intelligence in Medicine, Elsevier, Vol 127, May 2022

After studying these surveys, our contribution will involve studying genetic sequencing and imaging at the same time to predict breast cancer and to get more information that can help early diagnosis and treatment of breast cancer. We will also provide recommendations to researchers who wish to conduct research in this area. 3. Methodology Our target topic is breast cancer detection using deep learning. We ended up using around 80 of the most recent papers related to breast cancer treatment and diagnosis. Some of the papers examined only deep learning, while others used a combination of machine learning and deep learning. In our search process, we mainly used the Scopus database to obtain the articles. This is to exclude nonrefereed publications However, in Figure 1, we state the distribution of selected papers among the existing databases. The top five databases are PubMed, ScienceDirect (Elsevier), IEEE, Springer and Nature.

The imaging modalities we considered were ultrasound, radiography, mammography and magnetic resonance imaging (MRI), as well as various types of gene expression and gene sequencing. In this research, we focused on papers that implement the breast cancer detection using the techniques of AI, as well as papers that predict breast cancer using both gene data and image data. We applied the following eligibility criteria on each paper: (1) The language is English; (2) The topic is related to breast cancer detection and treatment; (3) The paper discusses hybrid models of machine learning and deep learning; (4) The paper purely discusses deep learning; (5) The paper discusses genetic expression data; (6) The paper discusses imaging data; (7) Only journal and conference publications are retained; (8) Only medical or biomedical engineering publications are kept which are related to the topic. Please note that non-refereed publications were excluded from the study. Firstly, we recorded the main information such as the name of the paper, year of publication, the list of authors and the publisher. Then, we included some information to conduct the systematic review, such as the algorithm used and whether the paper discusses only deep learning or a hybrid between DL and ML, the recorded accuracy and other performance evaluation parameters, the dataset, the features, and many other columns. We answered our research questions using these criteria. 4. Results and Discussion In this systematic study, our initial search turned up 1,000 conference and journal papers. After eliminating duplicated papers and unrelated studies that were "purely medical or about cancer in general", we ended up with 80 papers related to both ML and DL.

In machine learning method, data and output is run on the computer to create a program :

1. Sparse compact incremental learning machine (SCILM) method A new approach was designed to resolve cancer classification problem on microarray gene expression data, which take advantage of correntropy cost that makes it robust against diverse noises and outliers. Moreover, since SCILM uses l1-norm of the weights, it has sparseness, which can be applied for gene selection purposes as well. Finally, due to compact structure, the method is capable of performing classification tasks in all of the cases with only one neuron in its hidden layer. The experimental analysis in this method was performed on 26 well-known microarray data sets regarding diverse kinds of cancers and the results showed that the strategy not only achieved significantly high accuracy but also accompanied with effectivity of each gene regarding the corresponding cancer .

2. Knowledge base system learning method A new knowledge-based system for classification of cancer disease was proposed using clustering, noise removal, and classification techniques. Expectation Maximization (EM) was used as a clustering method to cluster the data in similar groups. Classification and Regression Trees (CART) were used to generate the fuzzy rules to be used for the classification of cancer disease in the knowledge-based system of fuzzy rule-based reasoning method. To overcome the multicollinearity issue, Principal Component Analysis (PCA) was incorporated in the current knowledge-based system. Experimental results on Wisconsin Diagnostic Breast Cancer and Mammographic mass datasets showed that current approach remarkably improves the prediction accuracy of breast cancer. The knowledge-based system can be used .

3. Gauss-Newton representation based learning method A novel Gauss-Newton representation based algorithm (GNRBA) for breast cancer classification. It uses the sparse representation with training sample selection. Until now, sparse representation has been successfully applied in pattern recognition only. This method introduces a novel Gauss-Newton based approach to find the optimal weights for the training samples for classification. In addition, it evaluates the sparsity in a computationally efficient way as compared to the conventional l1-norm method. The effectiveness of the GNRBA is examined on the Wisconsin Breast Cancer Database (WBCD) and the Wisconsin Diagnosis Breast Cancer (WDBC) database from the UCI Machine Learning repository. Various performance measures like classification accuracy, sensitivity, specificity, confusion matrices, a statistical test and the area under the receiver operating characteristic (AUC) are reported to show the superiority of the proposed method as compared to classical models [17].

4. Gene expression learning method Studying the characteristics of thousands of genes simultaneously offered a deep insight into cancer classification problem. It introduced an abundant amount of data ready to be explored. It has also been applied in a wide range of applications such as drug discovery, cancer prediction and diagnosis which is a very important issue for cancer treatment . Besides, it helps in understanding the function of genes and the interaction between genes in

normal and abnormal conditions . That is done by monitoring the behavior of genes, gene expression data under different conditions. Ensemble classifiers increase not only the performance of the classification, but also the confidence of the results. The motivations beyond using ensemble classifiers are that the results are less dependent on peculiarities of a single training set and because the ensemble system outperforms the performance of the best base classifier in the ensemble [19].

5. Ensemble predictive modeling framework learning method Molecular changes often precede clinical presentation of diseases and can be useful surrogates with potential to assist in informed clinical decision making. Recent studies have demonstrated the usefulness of modeling approaches such as classification that can predict the clinical outcomes from molecular expression profiles. While useful, a majority of these approaches implicitly use all molecular markers as features in the classification process often resulting in sparse high-dimensional projection of the samples often comparable to that of the sample size. Ensemble classification approach is used for predicting good and poorprognosis breast cancer samples from their molecular expression profiles [20]. In contrast to traditional

single and ensemble classifiers, the proposed approach uses multiple base classifiers with varying feature sets obtained from two-dimensional projection of the samples in conjunction with a majority voting strategy for predicting the class labels .

In contrast to earlier implementation, base classifiers in the ensembles are chosen based on maximal sensitivity and minimal redundancy by choosing only those with low average cosine distance. The resulting ensemble sets are subsequently modeled as undirected graphs. Performance of four different classification algorithms is shown to be better within the proposed ensemble framework in contrast to using them as traditional single classifier systems. Design of an efficient ensemble predictive modeling classification framework for prediction of breast density class .

6. Convolution neural network learning method Deep convolutional neural networks (CNNs) were designed to obtain more discriminative description of cancer tissues. Benefiting from the discriminative representation, metric learning layers are proposed to further improve performance of the deep structure. The bestperforming model restricts the depth of back I J Mutil Re App St Volume 1 Issue 1, 2017 PP. 1-8 6|Page propagation of joint training in only the metric learning layers. Relation between metric learning layers and tradition CNNs structures seems like parasitism relationship between species, where one species, the parasite, benefits at the expense of the other . Therefore, the method is named as parasitic metric learning net. To confirm veracity of this method, classification experiments on breast mass images of two widely used databases were performed . Comparing performance of the current method with traditional ones, competitive results were achieved. Meanwhile, the parameter updating strategy for parasitic metric net may inspire a way of improving performance of a pre-trained CNNs model on particular medical image processing or other computer vision tasks . Training pipeline of the proposed parasitic metric learning net .We discussed the concepts of machine learning while we outlined their application in cancer prediction/prognosis. Most of the studies that have been proposed the last years and focus on the development of predictive models using supervised machine learning methods and classification algorithms aiming to predict valid disease outcomes. Based on the analysis of their results, it is evident that the integration of multidimensional heterogeneous data, combined with the application of different techniques for feature selection and classification can provide promising tools for inference in the cancer domain.

EXPERIMENT AND METHODOLOGY :.

1 Data-sets A malignant tumour that has developed from cells of the breast is breast cancer. Although some of the scientifically known risk factors (i.e. ageing, genetic risk factors, family history, menstrual periods, not having children, obesity) that increase a woman's chance of developing breast cancer, the exact causes or some of these risk factors that causes cells to become cancerous are not exactly known by them. Research is under way to learn more and scientists are making great progress in understanding how certain changes in DNA can cause normal breast cells to become cancerous. This part of the project includes the research about the available dataset that can be used for the project. The initial dataset that we planned on working had certain drawbacks. CBIS-DDSM dataset: Neither the analytics nor the experimental validation of the data were sufficient to move forward with the project. There was no exact data regarding the classification of tumours into benign and malignant in case of scan images of patients.

One the most important demerit of this dataset was the improper organization of data and huge redundant records which can cause glitches in the training process. Hence it was concluded that evaluation based on detection rate and accuracy levels with this data-set is not appropriate. Breast cancer Wisconsin data-set: This dataset was a text type data-set which had a classified set of data into malignant and benign tumours based on the cell features threshold values for various features like cell radius, perimeter, area, symmetry and other such International Research Journal of Engineering and Technology . We didn't go for this data-set since we planned on a better version of cancer detection model which focused on images

2 Pre-processing data Data preprocessing is a data mining technique that is used for filter data in a usable format. Because the real-world data-set is almost available in different formats. It's not available as per our requirement so it must fit the data-set in an understandable format. Data pre processing is a proven method of resolving such issues. Data pre-processing converts the data-set into usable format for pre-processing. We have used a standardization method to pre- process the data-set. Encoder Method: Label Encoder is an efficient tool for encoding the levels of the categorical features into numeric values. Label Encoder encode labels with value between 0 and classes -1. All our categorical features are encoded. In this paper we have classified malignant and Benign in diagnosis with 0 and 1. After encoding the dataset we have applied a neural network on these dataset and achieved accuracy.

3 Normalizer Method Normalization is a better technique to use when distribution of the data is unknown.. Data normalization is the process of rescaling one and more attributes to the range of 0 to 1. This means that the largest value for each attribute is 1 and the smallest value is 0. After applying the Label Encoder method all dataset is converted into numeric dataset. Because Label Encoder encodes all string label dataset into numeric dataset. Normalization process is known to work on numeric dataset. So after normalized data we have applied a neural network on that dataset and achieved accuracy. But again accuracy is not yet adequate. So we have applied the next process for pre-processing.

.4. Convolutional Neural Network Convolutional Neural Network is a type of neural network technique which has proven to be specifically efficient with image recognition and classification. The input is a tensor with shape (number of images) x (image width) x (image height) x (image depth) in the programming CNN. Then the image becomes abstracted to a feature map, with shape (number of images) x (feature map width) x (feature map height) x (feature map channels)after passing through a convolutional layer. The following attributes are expected in a convolutional layer within a neural network : • Width and height (hyper-parameters) defined by convolutional kernels. • The number of input channels and output channels (hyper-parameter). • The number channels (depth) of the input feature map must be equal to depth of the Convolution filter (the input channels) The convolution of input and passing its result to the next layer is done by Convolutional layers. This is similar to the response of a neuron in the visual cortex to a specific stimulus. Each and every convolutional neuron processes data only for its receptive field. It is not practical to apply this architecture to images, even though fully connected feed forward neural networks can be used to learn features as well as classify data. Due to the very large input sizes related with images, a very high number of neurons would be required, even in a simplistic architecture which is not very deep, where each

pixel is a relevant variable. For example,in the second layer, a fully connected layer for an image of size 100 x 100 has 10,000 weights for each neuron. A way out to this issue is provided by the convolution operation by decreasing the number of free parameters, allowing the network to be even deeper with keeping the parameters few. Taking an example, irrespective of image size, tiling regions of size 5 x 5, each with the same shared weights, requires only 25 learnable parameters. If went by this, back propagation resolves the exploding or vanishing gradients difficulty in training traditional multi-layer neural networks with many layers. ReLU is the abbreviation of rectified linear unit, which applies the non-saturating activation functionf(x)=max(0,x). It successfully removes negative values from an activation map by setting them to zero. The nonlinear properties of the overall network and the decision function without affecting the receptive fields of the convolution layer are increased by it. Other functions are also used to extend nonlinearity, for instance the saturating hyperbolic tangent f(x)=tanh(x), f(x)=|tanh(x)| and the sigmoid function sigma(x)=(1+e^- x)^-1 . Since it trains the neural network several times faster without a large kr significant penalty to generalization accuracy, ReLU is preferred a lot more than the other functions.

5. Graphical User Interface The final part of the project includes a graphic user interface(GUI) which will act as a platform to feed fresh cell images for the module to detect whether the given image is cancerous or non cancerous. For this we use Flask. Flask is a web application framework which is written in python. It means by using flask,with the help of the tools, libraries and technologies provided by it , a complete web application can be built. This specific web application can be anything from wiki, a web page, a blog to something as big as a commercial website or a webbased major application. Flask also supports extensions that can add application details and characteristics as if they were implemented in Flask . It has proven to be a significant tool for learning web development basics and best techniques along with the main elements of a web International Research Journal of Engineering and Technology framework that are regular to almost all frameworks. Using all these components a GUI is created which will help in the classification of a new image.

GUI 5. MODEL IMPLEMENTATION Neural Network algorithm has been applied on the dataset in this stage. Neural network here works like a human biological method. In which we have to provide the input and get the output. But in these two layers, some hidden layers are present and it becomes mandatory that some additional process must be added before calculating the final output. These added units of bias, some of additional hidden layers, calculate the activation function and the final output is generated. The following parameters for calculating and training the model have been used in this model. Fig -4: Neural Network Functionality Fig shows the basic functionality of the neural network in which after the fixed position the neurons are fired that is called threshold condition. Table -1: Parameters in CCN model Parameters used in CCN model Number of inputs 512 Number of neurons 512 Activation function Relu Number of epochs 10 6. RESULTS AND DISCUSSION In this paper we have proposed a Deep Learning with Neural Network algorithm for diagnosis and detection of breast cancer. For pre-processing breast cancer dataset , we have used the standardization method . Then we have implemented a neural network algorithm and achieved 87.64% accuracy. By using breast-histopathology-images we tested 1728 images and received 87.64% which shows promising results as compared to other machine learning algorithms. Fig -5: Result of model 7. CONCLUSIONS

Cancer detection using machine learning is a system that mainly targets the early detection of cancer. With the ever increasing surge in the number of cancer diagnosis there is a need for better technology that increases the chance of survival. Hence we aim to use machine learning for early diagnosis which eventually increases the survival rate. For this, we have fed the machine with categorized data sets of malignant and benign cell images and for better results we have also shuffled these images within themselves and then have successfully trained the machine with malignant and benign data sets after which successful testing is performed with an unknown data set.

Breast cancer is one of the major causes of death in women around the world. According to the American cancer society, 41,760 women and more than 500 men died from breast cancer recently1. Breast cancer occurs in four main types: normal, benign, in-situ carcinoma and invasive carcinoma [. A benign tumor involves a minor change in the breast structure. It is not harmful and does not classify as a harmful cancer. In cases of in-situ carcinoma, the cancer is only in the mammary duct lobule system and does not affect other organs. This type is not dangerous and can be treated if diagnosed early. Invasive carcinoma is considered to be the most dangerous type of breast cancer, as it can spread to all other organs. According to the authors in [1], breast cancer can be detected using several methods including X-ray mammography, ultrasound (US), Computed Tomography (CT), Portion Emission Tomography (PET), Magnetic Resonance Imaging (MRI) and breast temperature measurement. Usually, the golden standard is a pathological diagnosis for detecting breast cancer. This involves an image analysis of the removed tissue, which is stained in the lab to increase visibility. Hematoxylin and Eosin (H&E) are commonly used for the staining process. Breast cancer can be diagnosed using one of two approaches: histopathological image analysis or genomics. Histopathological images are microscopic images of breast tissue that are extremely useful in early treatment of the cancer. As for genomics, the authors in stated that radio1 https://www.cancer.org/ Artificial Intelligence in Medicine, Elsevier, Vol 127, May 2022 genomics is an emerging research field focusing on multi-scale associations between medical imaging and gene expression data. Radio-genomics provide both radiological and genetic features that can enhance diagnosis. It can analyze tissues at the molecular level, helping with prediction and early detection of cancer. The main difference between imaging information and radio-genomics is the critical knowledge gap between imaging at the tissue level and analyzing the underlying molecular and genetic disease biomarkers. As imaging is less precise, it may lead to over- or under-treatment. While radio-genomics is much more effective than histopathological imaging, it is rarely used because the process involves datasets that are very expensive and require high computational power. As a result, a limited number of labs conduct radio-genomics experiments [.

This research paper addresses the following research questions and highlights the deep learning models, looking at their performance, the datasets used and possibilities for breast cancer classification and detection. 1. Which deep learning models perform most effectively? We will compare deep learning models with classical machine learning models to compare their performance. We will also list the performance metrics used. 2. What are the most used features for breast cancer classification? How are these features selected and extracted? We will observe the most important features that contribute to breast cancer classification, and the methods used to extract these features. 3. What datasets are available for both gene sequencing and MRI? What feature selection and extraction methods are

used? We will list and discuss all public and private datasets for gene sequencing and MRI imaging data. We will also list some of the methods used to select and extract the features. 4. Comparing gene sequence data with image data, for breast cancer detection problem, what are the drawbacks, challenges, and advantages? We will compare imaging and gene sequencing as they relate to breast cancer detection, using a tabular presentation to highlight the main differences between the two approaches. This is structured as follows:

Section 2 presents related work which includes surveys conducted in breast cancer area.

Section 3 explains the methodology used to conduct this research.

Section 4 presents the obtained results and related discussions.

Lastly, Section 5 concludes the paper and suggests future research directions. 2. Related Work Many studies have been conducted about breast cancer detection through imaging or through genomics. However, to the best of our knowledge, no research has been conducted including both techniques. The authors in [1] summarized the various techniques used to classify breast cancer using histopathological image analysis (HIA) based on different architectures of Artificial Neural Networks (ANN). The authors Artificial Intelligence in Medicine, Elsevier, Vol 127, May 2022 grouped their work according to the applied dataset. They arranged it in ascending chronological order. This work found that ANNs were first used in the field of HIA around 2012. ANNs and PNNs were the most frequently applied algorithms. However, in feature extraction, most of the work used textural and morphological features. It was clear that Deep CNNs were quite effective for early detection and diagnosis of breast cancer, leading to more successful treatment. Prediction of Non-Communicable Diseases (NCDs) was conducted using many algorithms.

In this the authors compared the performance of various classification algorithms. The classification algorithms were performed on eight NCD datasets using eight classification algorithms and a 10-fold crossvalidation method. These were evaluated using AUC as an indicator of accuracy. The authors stated that the NCD datasets have noisy data and irrelevant attributes. KNN, SVM and NN proved to be robust to this noise. In addition, they stated that the irrelevant attribute problem can be handled with some pre-processing techniques to improve the accuracy rate. Natural inspired computing (NIC) algorithms have been designed and applied to diagnose various human disorders. The authors in [3)introduced five insect-based NIC algorithms used for diagnosing diabetes and cancer. The authors found that it achieved a high level of performance in detecting different types of cancer (breast, lung, prostate and ovarian). To be more specific, breast cancer was detected using a hybridization of the guided ABC and neural networks. The authors also developed a highly effective methodology of detecting diabetes and leukemia. They concluded that the hybridization of NICs with other classification algorithms produces more precise and promising results. They mentioned that more work is required to detect different stages of diabetes and cancer.

In [4], the authors demonstrated the effectiveness of NNs in the classification of cancer diagnoses, especially in the initial stages. According to their study, the majority of NNs have shown promise in detecting tumor cells. However, the imaging approach requires high computational capacity to preprocess the images.

In [5], the authors reviewed different machine learning, deep learning and data mining algorithms related to breast cancer prediction. Several research papers on breast cancer were reviewed, with a total of 27 papers in machine learning, 4 papers in ensemble techniques and 8 papers in deep learning techniques. The authors mentioned that most of the papers used imaging, while only a few papers used genetics. The main algorithms used to predict breast cancer using genetics were SVM, decision tree and random forest. However, imaging techniques used several algorithms such as CNNs and Naïve Bayes. On the other hand, the authors

in [6] focused on gene mutation for detecting breast cancer. They mentioned that the gene prediction classification phase aims to carry out gene annotation, gene finding and gene mutation detection to ascertain the presence or absence of a cancer. They concluded that several methods can be used including regression, probability models, SVMs, NNs and deep learning. They also mentioned the many opportunities available to capture the relationship between nucleotide and feature extraction, since DNA sequencing involves a large amount of data in the form of a string sequence.

In [7], the authors examined recent studies applying deep learning to breast cancer with different imaging modalities. They organized these studies using the aspects of dataset, architecture, application and evaluation. They focused on deep learning frameworks developed in three breast imaging modalities (ultrasound, mammography and MRI). In their work, they attempted to provide state-of-the-art findings about breast cancer imaging utilizing DLR-based CAD systems. Their study included private datasets and classification using CNNs. Artificial Intelligence in Medicine, Elsevier, Vol 127, May 2022

After studying these surveys, our contribution will involve studying genetic sequencing and imaging at the same time to predict breast cancer and to get more information that can help early diagnosis and treatment of breast cancer. We will also provide recommendations to researchers who wish to conduct research in this area. 3. Methodology Our target topic is breast cancer detection using deep learning. We ended up using around 80 of the most recent papers related to breast cancer treatment and diagnosis. Some of the papers examined only deep learning, while others used a combination of machine learning and deep learning. In our search process, we mainly used the Scopus database to obtain the articles. This is to exclude nonrefereed publications However, in Figure 1, we state the distribution of selected papers among the existing databases. The top five databases are PubMed, ScienceDirect (Elsevier), IEEE, Springer and Nature.

The imaging modalities we considered were ultrasound, radiography, mammography and magnetic resonance imaging (MRI), as well as various types of gene expression and gene sequencing. In this research, we focused on papers that implement the breast cancer detection using the techniques of AI, as well as papers that predict breast cancer using both gene data and image data. We applied the following eligibility criteria on each paper: (1) The language is English; (2) The topic is related to breast cancer detection and treatment; (3) The paper discusses hybrid models of machine learning and deep learning; (4) The paper purely discusses deep learning; (5) The paper discusses genetic expression data; (6) The paper discusses imaging data; (7) Only journal and conference publications are retained; (8) Only medical or biomedical engineering publications are kept which are related to the topic. Please

note that non-refereed publications were excluded from the study. Firstly, we recorded the main information such as the name of the paper, year of publication, the list of authors and the publisher. Then, we included some information to conduct the systematic review, such as the algorithm used and whether the paper discusses only deep learning or a hybrid between DL and ML, the recorded accuracy and other performance evaluation parameters, the dataset, the features, and many other columns. We answered our research questions using these criteria. 4. Results and Discussion In this systematic study, our initial search turned up 1,000 conference and journal papers. After eliminating duplicated papers and unrelated studies that were "purely medical or about cancer in general", we ended up with 80 papers related to both ML and DL.

In machine learning method, data and output is run on the computer to create a program :

1. Sparse compact incremental learning machine (SCILM) method A new approach was designed to resolve cancer classification problem on microarray gene expression data, which take advantage of correntropy cost that makes it robust against diverse noises and outliers. Moreover, since SCILM uses l1-norm of the weights, it has sparseness, which can be applied for gene selection purposes as well. Finally, due to compact structure, the method is capable of performing classification tasks in all of the cases with only one neuron in its hidden layer. The experimental analysis in this method was performed on 26 well-known microarray data sets regarding diverse kinds of cancers and the results showed that the strategy not only achieved significantly high accuracy but also accompanied with effectivity of each gene regarding the corresponding cancer .

2. Knowledge base system learning method A new knowledge-based system for classification of cancer disease was proposed using clustering, noise removal, and classification techniques. Expectation Maximization (EM) was used as a clustering method to cluster the data in similar groups. Classification and Regression Trees (CART) were used to generate the fuzzy rules to be used for the classification of cancer disease in the knowledge-based system of fuzzy rule-based reasoning method. To overcome the multicollinearity issue, Principal Component Analysis (PCA) was incorporated in the current knowledge-based system. Experimental results on Wisconsin Diagnostic Breast Cancer and Mammographic mass datasets showed that current approach remarkably improves the prediction accuracy of breast cancer. The knowledge-based system can be used .

3. Gauss-Newton representation based learning method A novel Gauss-Newton representation based algorithm (GNRBA) for breast cancer classification. It uses the sparse representation with training sample selection. Until now, sparse representation has been successfully applied in pattern recognition only. This method introduces a novel Gauss-Newton based approach to find the optimal weights for the training samples for classification. In addition, it evaluates the sparsity in a computationally efficient way as compared to the conventional l1-norm method. The effectiveness of the GNRBA is examined on the Wisconsin Breast Cancer Database (WBCD) and the Wisconsin Diagnosis Breast Cancer (WDBC) database from the UCI Machine Learning repository. Various performance measures like classification accuracy, sensitivity, specificity, confusion matrices, a statistical test and the area under the receiver operating characteristic (AUC) are reported to show the superiority of the proposed method as compared to classical models [17].

4. Gene expression learning method Studying the characteristics of thousands of genes simultaneously offered a deep insight into cancer classification problem. It introduced an abundant amount of data ready to be explored. It has also been applied in a wide range of applications such as drug discovery, cancer prediction and diagnosis which is a very important issue for cancer treatment . Besides, it helps in understanding the function of genes and the interaction between genes in

normal and abnormal conditions . That is done by monitoring the behavior of genes, gene expression data under different conditions. Ensemble classifiers increase not only the performance of the classification, but also the confidence of the results. The motivations beyond using ensemble classifiers are that the results are less dependent on peculiarities of a single training set and because the ensemble system outperforms the performance of the best base classifier in the ensemble [19].

5. Ensemble predictive modeling framework learning method Molecular changes often precede clinical presentation of diseases and can be useful surrogates with potential to assist in informed clinical decision making. Recent studies have demonstrated the usefulness of modeling approaches such as classification that can predict the clinical outcomes from molecular expression profiles. While useful, a majority of these approaches implicitly use all molecular markers as features in the classification process often resulting in sparse high-dimensional projection of the samples often comparable to that of the sample size. Ensemble classification approach is used for predicting good and poorprognosis breast cancer samples from their molecular expression profiles [20]. In contrast to traditional single and ensemble classifiers, the proposed approach uses multiple base classifiers with varying feature sets obtained from two-dimensional projection of the samples in conjunction with a majority voting strategy for predicting the class labels .

In contrast to earlier implementation, base classifiers in the ensembles are chosen based on maximal sensitivity and minimal redundancy by choosing only those with low average cosine distance. The resulting ensemble sets are subsequently modeled as undirected graphs. Performance of four different classification algorithms is shown to be better within the proposed ensemble framework in contrast to using them as traditional single classifier systems. Design of an efficient ensemble predictive modeling classification framework for prediction of breast density class .

6. Convolution neural network learning method Deep convolutional neural networks (CNNs) were designed to obtain more discriminative description of cancer tissues. Benefiting from the discriminative representation, metric learning layers are proposed to further improve performance of the deep structure. The bestperforming model restricts the depth of back I J Mutil Re App St Volume 1 Issue 1, 2017 PP. 1-8 6|Page propagation of joint training in only the metric learning layers. Relation between metric learning layers and tradition CNNs structures seems like parasitism relationship between species, where one species, the parasite, benefits at the expense of the other . Therefore, the method is named as parasitic metric learning net. To confirm veracity of this method, classification experiments on breast mass images of two widely used databases were performed . Comparing performance of the current method with traditional ones, competitive results were achieved. Meanwhile, the parameter updating strategy for parasitic metric net may inspire a way of improving performance of a pre-trained CNNs model on

particular medical image processing or other computer vision tasks . Training pipeline of the proposed parasitic metric learning net .We discussed the concepts of machine learning while we outlined their application in cancer prediction/prognosis. Most of the studies that have been proposed the last years and focus on the development of predictive models using supervised machine learning methods and classification algorithms aiming to predict valid disease outcomes. Based on the analysis of their results, it is evident that the integration of multidimensional heterogeneous data, combined with the application of different techniques for feature selection and classification can provide promising tools for inference in the cancer domain.

EXPERIMENT AND METHODOLOGY :.

1 Data-sets A malignant tumour that has developed from cells of the breast is breast cancer. Although some of the scientifically known risk factors (i.e. ageing, genetic risk factors, family history, menstrual periods, not having children, obesity) that increase a woman's chance of developing breast cancer, the exact causes or some of these risk factors that causes cells to become cancerous are not exactly known by them. Research is under way to learn more and scientists are making great progress in understanding how certain changes in DNA can cause normal breast cells to become cancerous. This part of the project includes the research about the available dataset that can be used for the project. The initial dataset that we planned on working had certain drawbacks. CBIS-DDSM dataset: Neither the analytics nor the experimental validation of the data were sufficient to move forward with the project. There was no exact data regarding the classification of tumours into benign and malignant in case of scan images of patients. One the most important demerit of this dataset was the improper organization of data and huge redundant records which can cause glitches in the training process. Hence it was concluded that evaluation based on detection rate and accuracy levels with this data-set is not appropriate. Breast cancer Wisconsin data-set: This dataset was a text type data-set which had a classified set of data into malignant and benign tumours based on the cell features threshold values for various features like cell radius, perimeter, area, symmetry and other such International Research Journal of Engineering and Technology . We didn't go for this data-set since we planned on a better version of cancer detection model which focused on images

2 Pre-processing data Data preprocessing is a data mining technique that is used for filter data in a usable format. Because the real-world data-set is almost available in different formats. It's not available as per our requirement so it must fit the data-set in an understandable format. Data pre processing is a proven method of resolving such issues. Data pre-processing converts the data-set into usable format for pre-processing. We have used a standardization method to pre- process the data-set. Encoder Method: Label Encoder is an efficient tool for encoding the levels of the categorical features into numeric values. Label Encoder encode labels with value between 0 and classes -1. All our categorical features are encoded. In this paper we have classified malignant and Benign in diagnosis with 0 and 1. After encoding the dataset we have applied a neural network on these dataset and achieved accuracy.

3 Normalizer Method Normalization is a better technique to use when distribution of the data is unknown.. Data normalization is the process of rescaling one and more attributes to the range of 0 to 1. This means that the largest value for each attribute is 1 and the smallest value is 0. After applying the Label Encoder method all dataset

is converted into numeric dataset. Because Label Encoder encodes all string label dataset into numeric dataset. Normalization process is known to work on numeric dataset. So after normalized data we have applied a neural network on that dataset and achieved accuracy. But again accuracy is not yet adequate. So we have applied the next process for pre-processing.

.4. Convolutional Neural Network Convolutional Neural Network is a type of neural network technique which has proven to be specifically efficient with image recognition and classification. The input is a tensor with shape (number of images) x (image width) x (image height) x (image depth) in the programming CNN. Then the image becomes abstracted to a feature map, with shape (number of images) x (feature map width) x (feature map height) x (feature map channels)after passing through a convolutional layer. The following attributes are expected in a convolutional layer within a neural network : • Width and height (hyper-parameters) defined by convolutional kernels. • The number of input channels and output channels (hyper-parameter). • The number channels (depth) of the input feature map must be equal to depth of the Convolution filter (the input channels) The convolution of input and passing its result to the next layer is done by Convolutional layers. This is similar to the response of a neuron in the visual cortex to a specific stimulus. Each and every convolutional neuron processes data only for its receptive field. It is not practical to apply this architecture to images, even though fully connected feed forward neural networks can be used to learn features as well as classify data. Due to the very large input sizes related with images, a very high number of neurons would be required, even in a simplistic architecture which is not very deep, where each pixel is a relevant variable. For example,in the second layer, a fully connected layer for an image of size 100 x 100 has 10,000 weights for each neuron. A way out to this issue is provided by the convolution operation by decreasing the number of free parameters, allowing the network to be even deeper with keeping the parameters few. Taking an example, irrespective of image size, tiling regions of size 5 x 5, each with the same shared weights, requires only 25 learnable parameters. If went by this, back propagation resolves the exploding or vanishing gradients difficulty in training traditional multi-layer neural networks with many layers. ReLU is the abbreviation of rectified linear unit, which applies the non-saturating activation functionf(x)=max(0,x). It successfully removes negative values from an activation map by setting them to zero. The nonlinear properties of the overall network and the decision function without affecting the receptive fields of the convolution layer are increased by it. Other functions are also used to extend nonlinearity, for instance the saturating hyperbolic tangent f(x)=tanh(x), f(x)=|tanh(x)| and the sigmoid function sigma(x)=(1+e^- x)^-1 . Since it trains the neural network several times faster without a large kr significant penalty to generalization accuracy, ReLU is preferred a lot more than the other functions.

5. Graphical User Interface The final part of the project includes a graphic user interface(GUI) which will act as a platform to feed fresh cell images for the module to detect whether the given image is cancerous or non cancerous. For this we use Flask. Flask is a web application framework which is written in python. It means by using flask,with the help of the tools, libraries and technologies provided by it , a complete web application can be built. This specific web application can be anything from wiki, a web page, a blog to something as big as a commercial website or a webbased major application. Flask also supports extensions that can add application details and characteristics as if

they were implemented in Flask . It has proven to be a significant tool for learning web development basics and best techniques along with the main elements of a web International Research Journal of Engineering and Technology framework that are regular to almost all frameworks. Using all these components a GUI is created which will help in the classification of a new image.

GUI 5. MODEL IMPLEMENTATION Neural Network algorithm has been applied on the dataset in this stage. Neural network here works like a human biological method. In which we have to provide the input and get the output. But in these two layers, some hidden layers are present and it becomes mandatory that some additional process must be added before calculating the final output. These added units of bias, some of additional hidden layers, calculate the activation function and the final output is generated. The following parameters for calculating and training the model have been used in this model. Fig -4: Neural Network Functionality Fig shows the basic functionality of the neural network in which after the fixed position the neurons are fired that is called threshold condition. Table -1: Parameters in CCN model Parameters used in CCN model Number of inputs 512 Number of neurons 512 Activation function Relu Number of epochs 10 6. RESULTS AND DISCUSSION In this paper we have proposed a Deep Learning with Neural Network algorithm for diagnosis and detection of breast cancer. For pre-processing breast cancer dataset , we have used the standardization method . Then we have implemented a neural network algorithm and achieved 87.64% accuracy. By using breast-histopathology-images we tested 1728 images and received 87.64% which shows promising results as compared to other machine learning algorithms. Fig -5: Result of model 7. CONCLUSIONS Cancer detection using machine learning is a system that mainly targets the early detection of cancer. With the ever increasing surge in the number of cancer diagnosis there is a need for better technology that increases the chance of survival. Hence we aim to use machine learning for early diagnosis which eventually increases the survival rate. For this, we have fed the machine with categorized data sets of malignant and benign cell images and for better results we have also shuffled these images within themselves and then have successfully trained the machine with malignant and benign data sets after which successful testing is performed with an unknown data set.

Breast cancer is one of the major causes of death in women around the world. According to the American cancer society, 41,760 women and more than 500 men died from breast cancer recently1. Breast cancer occurs in four main types: normal, benign, in-situ carcinoma and invasive carcinoma [. A benign tumor involves a minor change in the breast structure. It is not harmful and does not classify as a harmful cancer. In cases of in-situ carcinoma, the cancer is only in the mammary duct lobule system and does not affect other organs. This type is not dangerous and can be treated if diagnosed early. Invasive carcinoma is considered to be the most dangerous type of breast cancer, as it can spread to all other organs. According to the authors in [1], breast cancer can be detected using several methods including X-ray mammography, ultrasound (US), Computed Tomography (CT), Portion Emission Tomography (PET), Magnetic Resonance Imaging (MRI) and breast temperature measurement. Usually, the golden standard is a pathological diagnosis for detecting breast cancer. This involves an image analysis of the removed tissue, which is stained in the lab to increase visibility. Hematoxylin and Eosin (H&E) are commonly used for the staining process. Breast cancer can be diagnosed using one of two approaches: histopathological image analysis or genomics.

Histopathological images are microscopic images of breast tissue that are extremely useful in early treatment of the cancer. As for genomics, the authors in stated that radio1 https://www.cancer.org/ Artificial Intelligence in Medicine, Elsevier, Vol 127, May 2022 genomics is an emerging research field focusing on multi-scale associations between medical imaging and gene expression data. Radio-genomics provide both radiological and genetic features that can enhance diagnosis. It can analyze tissues at the molecular level, helping with prediction and early detection of cancer. The main difference between imaging information and radio-genomics is the critical knowledge gap between imaging at the tissue level and analyzing the underlying molecular and genetic disease biomarkers. As imaging is less precise, it may lead to over- or under-treatment. While radio-genomics is much more effective than histopathological imaging, it is rarely used because the process involves datasets that are very expensive and require high computational power. As a result, a limited number of labs conduct radio-genomics experiments [.

This research paper addresses the following research questions and highlights the deep learning models, looking at their performance, the datasets used and possibilities for breast cancer classification and detection. 1. Which deep learning models perform most effectively? We will compare deep learning models with classical machine learning models to compare their performance. We will also list the performance metrics used. 2. What are the most used features for breast cancer classification? How are these features selected and extracted? We will observe the most important features that contribute to breast cancer classification, and the methods used to extract these features. 3. What datasets are available for both gene sequencing and MRI? What feature selection and extraction methods are used? We will list and discuss all public and private datasets for gene sequencing and MRI imaging data. We will also list some of the methods used to select and extract the features. 4. Comparing gene sequence data with image data, for breast cancer detection problem, what are the drawbacks, challenges, and advantages? We will compare imaging and gene sequencing as they relate to breast cancer detection, using a tabular presentation to highlight the main differences between the two approaches. This is structured as follows:

Section 2 presents related work which includes surveys conducted in breast cancer area.

Section 3 explains the methodology used to conduct this research.

Section 4 presents the obtained results and related discussions.

Lastly, Section 5 concludes the paper and suggests future research directions. 2. Related Work Many studies have been conducted about breast cancer detection through imaging or through genomics. However, to the best of our knowledge, no research has been conducted including both techniques. The authors in [1] summarized the various techniques used to classify breast cancer using histopathological image analysis (HIA) based on different architectures of Artificial Neural Networks (ANN). The authors Artificial Intelligence in Medicine, Elsevier, Vol 127, May 2022 grouped their work according to the applied dataset. They arranged it in ascending chronological order. This work found that ANNs were first used in the field of HIA around 2012. ANNs and PNNs were the most frequently applied algorithms. However, in feature extraction, most of the work used textural and morphological features. It was clear that Deep CNNs were quite effective for early detection and diagnosis of breast cancer, leading to more successful treatment. Prediction of Non-Communicable Diseases (NCDs) was conducted using many algorithms.

In this the authors compared the performance of various classification algorithms. The classification algorithms were performed on eight NCD datasets using eight classification algorithms and a 10-fold crossvalidation method. These were evaluated using AUC as an indicator of accuracy. The authors stated that the NCD datasets have noisy data and irrelevant attributes. KNN, SVM and NN proved to be robust to this noise. In addition, they stated that the irrelevant attribute problem can be handled with some pre-processing techniques to improve the accuracy rate. Natural inspired computing (NIC) algorithms have been designed and applied to diagnose various human disorders. The authors in [3)introduced five insect-based NIC algorithms used for diagnosing diabetes and cancer. The authors found that it achieved a high level of performance in detecting different types of cancer (breast, lung, prostate and ovarian). To be more specific, breast cancer was detected using a hybridization of the guided ABC and neural networks. The authors also developed a highly effective methodology of detecting diabetes and leukemia. They concluded that the hybridization of NICs with other classification algorithms produces more precise and promising results. They mentioned that more work is required to detect different stages of diabetes and cancer.

In [4], the authors demonstrated the effectiveness of NNs in the classification of cancer diagnoses, especially in the initial stages. According to their study, the majority of NNs have shown promise in detecting tumor cells. However, the imaging approach requires high computational capacity to preprocess the images.

In [5], the authors reviewed different machine learning, deep learning and data mining algorithms related to breast cancer prediction. Several research papers on breast cancer were reviewed, with a total of 27 papers in machine learning, 4 papers in ensemble techniques and 8 papers in deep learning techniques. The authors mentioned that most of the papers used imaging, while only a few papers used genetics. The main algorithms used to predict breast cancer using genetics were SVM, decision tree and random forest. However, imaging techniques used several algorithms such as CNNs and Naïve Bayes. On the other hand, the authors

in [6] focused on gene mutation for detecting breast cancer. They mentioned that the gene prediction classification phase aims to carry out gene annotation, gene finding and gene mutation detection to ascertain the presence or absence of a cancer. They concluded that several methods can be used including regression, probability models, SVMs, NNs and deep learning. They also mentioned the many opportunities available to capture the relationship between nucleotide and feature extraction, since DNA sequencing involves a large amount of data in the form of a string sequence.

In [7], the authors examined recent studies applying deep learning to breast cancer with different imaging modalities. They organized these studies using the aspects of dataset, architecture, application and evaluation. They focused on deep learning frameworks developed in three breast imaging modalities (ultrasound, mammography and MRI). In their work, they attempted to provide state-of-the-art findings about breast cancer imaging utilizing DLR-based CAD systems. Their study included private datasets and classification using CNNs. Artificial Intelligence in Medicine, Elsevier, Vol 127, May 2022

After studying these surveys, our contribution will involve studying genetic sequencing and imaging at the same time to predict breast cancer and to get more information that can help early diagnosis and treatment of breast cancer. We will also provide recommendations to researchers who wish to conduct research in this area. 3. Methodology Our target topic is breast cancer detection using deep learning. We ended up using around 80 of the most recent papers related to breast cancer treatment and diagnosis. Some of the papers examined only deep learning, while others used a combination of machine learning and deep learning. In our search process, we mainly used the Scopus database to obtain the articles. This is to exclude nonrefereed publications However, in Figure 1, we state the distribution of selected papers among the existing databases. The top five databases are PubMed, ScienceDirect (Elsevier), IEEE, Springer and Nature.

The imaging modalities we considered were ultrasound, radiography, mammography and magnetic resonance imaging (MRI), as well as various types of gene expression and gene sequencing. In this research, we focused on papers that implement the breast cancer detection using the techniques of AI, as well as papers that predict breast cancer using both gene data and image data. We applied the following eligibility criteria on each paper: (1) The language is English; (2) The topic is related to breast cancer detection and treatment; (3) The paper discusses hybrid models of machine learning and deep learning; (4) The paper purely discusses deep learning; (5) The paper discusses genetic expression data; (6) The paper discusses imaging data; (7) Only journal and conference publications are retained; (8) Only medical or biomedical engineering publications are kept which are related to the topic. Please note that non-refereed publications were excluded from the study. Firstly, we recorded the main information such as the name of the paper, year of publication, the list of authors and the publisher. Then, we included some information to conduct the systematic review, such as the algorithm used and whether the paper discusses only deep learning or a hybrid between DL and ML, the recorded accuracy and other performance evaluation parameters, the dataset, the features, and many other columns. We answered our research questions using these criteria. 4. Results and Discussion In this systematic study, our initial search turned up 1,000 conference and journal papers. After eliminating duplicated papers and unrelated studies that were "purely medical or about cancer in general", we ended up with 80 papers related to both ML and DL.

In machine learning method, data and output is run on the computer to create a program :

1. Sparse compact incremental learning machine (SCILM) method A new approach was designed to resolve cancer classification problem on microarray gene expression data, which take advantage of correntropy cost that makes it robust against diverse noises and outliers. Moreover, since SCILM uses l1-norm of the weights, it has sparseness, which can be applied for gene selection purposes as well. Finally, due to compact structure, the method is capable of performing classification tasks in all of the cases with only one neuron in its hidden layer. The experimental analysis in this method was performed on 26 well-known microarray data sets regarding diverse kinds of cancers and the results showed that the strategy not only achieved significantly high accuracy but also accompanied with effectivity of each gene regarding the corresponding cancer .

2. Knowledge base system learning method A new knowledge-based system for classification of cancer disease was proposed using clustering, noise removal, and classification techniques. Expectation Maximization (EM) was used as a clustering method to cluster the data in similar groups. Classification and Regression Trees (CART) were used to generate the fuzzy rules to be used for the classification of cancer disease in the knowledge-based system of fuzzy rule-based reasoning method. To overcome the multicollinearity issue, Principal Component Analysis (PCA) was incorporated in the current knowledge-based system. Experimental results on Wisconsin Diagnostic Breast Cancer and Mammographic mass datasets showed that current approach remarkably improves the prediction accuracy of breast cancer. The knowledge-based system can be used .

3. Gauss-Newton representation based learning method A novel Gauss-Newton representation based algorithm (GNRBA) for breast cancer classification. It uses the sparse representation with training sample selection. Until now, sparse representation has been successfully applied in pattern recognition only. This method introduces a novel Gauss-Newton based approach to find the optimal weights for the training samples for classification. In addition, it evaluates the sparsity in a computationally efficient way as compared to the conventional l1-norm method. The effectiveness of the GNRBA is examined on the Wisconsin Breast Cancer Database (WBCD) and the Wisconsin Diagnosis Breast Cancer (WDBC) database from the UCI Machine Learning repository. Various performance measures like classification accuracy, sensitivity, specificity, confusion matrices, a statistical test and the area under the receiver operating characteristic (AUC) are reported to show the superiority of the proposed method as compared to classical models [17].

4. Gene expression learning method Studying the characteristics of thousands of genes simultaneously offered a deep insight into cancer classification problem. It introduced an abundant amount of data ready to be explored. It has also been applied in a wide range of applications such as drug discovery, cancer prediction and diagnosis which is a very important issue for cancer treatment . Besides, it helps in understanding the function of genes and the interaction between genes in

normal and abnormal conditions . That is done by monitoring the behavior of genes, gene expression data under different conditions. Ensemble classifiers increase not only the performance of the classification, but also the confidence of the results. The motivations beyond using ensemble classifiers are that the results are less dependent on peculiarities of a single training set and because the ensemble system outperforms the performance of the best base classifier in the ensemble [19].

5. Ensemble predictive modeling framework learning method Molecular changes often precede clinical presentation of diseases and can be useful surrogates with potential to assist in informed clinical decision making. Recent studies have demonstrated the usefulness of modeling approaches such as classification that can predict the clinical outcomes from molecular expression profiles. While useful, a majority of these approaches implicitly use all molecular markers as features in the classification process often resulting in sparse high-dimensional projection of the samples often comparable to that of the sample size. Ensemble classification approach is used for predicting good and poorprognosis breast cancer samples from their molecular expression profiles [20]. In contrast to traditional

single and ensemble classifiers, the proposed approach uses multiple base classifiers with varying feature sets obtained from two-dimensional projection of the samples in conjunction with a majority voting strategy for predicting the class labels .

In contrast to earlier implementation, base classifiers in the ensembles are chosen based on maximal sensitivity and minimal redundancy by choosing only those with low average cosine distance. The resulting ensemble sets are subsequently modeled as undirected graphs. Performance of four different classification algorithms is shown to be better within the proposed ensemble framework in contrast to using them as traditional single classifier systems. Design of an efficient ensemble predictive modeling classification framework for prediction of breast density class .

6. Convolution neural network learning method Deep convolutional neural networks (CNNs) were designed to obtain more discriminative description of cancer tissues. Benefiting from the discriminative representation, metric learning layers are proposed to further improve performance of the deep structure. The bestperforming model restricts the depth of back I J Mutil Re App St Volume 1 Issue 1, 2017 PP. 1-8 6|Page propagation of joint training in only the metric learning layers. Relation between metric learning layers and tradition CNNs structures seems like parasitism relationship between species, where one species, the parasite, benefits at the expense of the other . Therefore, the method is named as parasitic metric learning net. To confirm veracity of this method, classification experiments on breast mass images of two widely used databases were performed . Comparing performance of the current method with traditional ones, competitive results were achieved. Meanwhile, the parameter updating strategy for parasitic metric net may inspire a way of improving performance of a pre-trained CNNs model on particular medical image processing or other computer vision tasks . Training pipeline of the proposed parasitic metric learning net .We discussed the concepts of machine learning while we outlined their application in cancer prediction/prognosis. Most of the studies that have been proposed the last years and focus on the development of predictive models using supervised machine learning methods and classification algorithms aiming to predict valid disease outcomes. Based on the analysis of their results, it is evident that the integration of multidimensional heterogeneous data, combined with the application of different techniques for feature selection and classification can provide promising tools for inference in the cancer domain.

EXPERIMENT AND METHODOLOGY :.

1 Data-sets A malignant tumour that has developed from cells of the breast is breast cancer. Although some of the scientifically known risk factors (i.e. ageing, genetic risk factors, family history, menstrual periods, not having children, obesity) that increase a woman's chance of developing breast cancer, the exact causes or some of these risk factors that causes cells to become cancerous are not exactly known by them. Research is under way to learn more and scientists are making great progress in understanding how certain changes in DNA can cause normal breast cells to become cancerous. This part of the project includes the research about the available dataset that can be used for the project. The initial dataset that we planned on working had certain drawbacks. CBIS-DDSM dataset: Neither the analytics nor the experimental validation of the data were sufficient to move forward with the project. There was no exact data regarding the classification of tumours into benign and malignant in case of scan images of patients.

One the most important demerit of this dataset was the improper organization of data and huge redundant records which can cause glitches in the training process. Hence it was concluded that evaluation based on detection rate and accuracy levels with this data-set is not appropriate. Breast cancer Wisconsin data-set: This dataset was a text type data-set which had a classified set of data into malignant and benign tumours based on the cell features threshold values for various features like cell radius, perimeter, area, symmetry and other such International Research Journal of Engineering and Technology . We didn't go for this data-set since we planned on a better version of cancer detection model which focused on images

2 Pre-processing data Data preprocessing is a data mining technique that is used for filter data in a usable format. Because the real-world data-set is almost available in different formats. It's not available as per our requirement so it must fit the data-set in an understandable format. Data pre processing is a proven method of resolving such issues. Data pre-processing converts the data-set into usable format for pre-processing. We have used a standardization method to pre- process the data-set. Encoder Method: Label Encoder is an efficient tool for encoding the levels of the categorical features into numeric values. Label Encoder encode labels with value between 0 and classes -1. All our categorical features are encoded. In this paper we have classified malignant and Benign in diagnosis with 0 and 1. After encoding the dataset we have applied a neural network on these dataset and achieved accuracy.

3 Normalizer Method Normalization is a better technique to use when distribution of the data is unknown.. Data normalization is the process of rescaling one and more attributes to the range of 0 to 1. This means that the largest value for each attribute is 1 and the smallest value is 0. After applying the Label Encoder method all dataset is converted into numeric dataset. Because Label Encoder encodes all string label dataset into numeric dataset. Normalization process is known to work on numeric dataset. So after normalized data we have applied a neural network on that dataset and achieved accuracy. But again accuracy is not yet adequate. So we have applied the next process for pre-processing.

.4. Convolutional Neural Network Convolutional Neural Network is a type of neural network technique which has proven to be specifically efficient with image recognition and classification. The input is a tensor with shape (number of images) x (image width) x (image height) x (image depth) in the programming CNN. Then the image becomes abstracted to a feature map, with shape (number of images) x (feature map width) x (feature map height) x (feature map channels)after passing through a convolutional layer. The following attributes are expected in a convolutional layer within a neural network : • Width and height (hyper-parameters) defined by convolutional kernels. • The number of input channels and output channels (hyper-parameter). • The number channels (depth) of the input feature map must be equal to depth of the Convolution filter (the input channels) The convolution of input and passing its result to the next layer is done by Convolutional layers. This is similar to the response of a neuron in the visual cortex to a specific stimulus. Each and every convolutional neuron processes data only for its receptive field. It is not practical to apply this architecture to images, even though fully connected feed forward neural networks can be used to learn features as well as classify data. Due to the very large input sizes related with images, a very high number of neurons would be required, even in a simplistic architecture which is not very deep, where each

pixel is a relevant variable. For example,in the second layer, a fully connected layer for an image of size 100 x 100 has 10,000 weights for each neuron. A way out to this issue is provided by the convolution operation by decreasing the number of free parameters, allowing the network to be even deeper with keeping the parameters few. Taking an example, irrespective of image size, tiling regions of size 5 x 5, each with the same shared weights, requires only 25 learnable parameters. If went by this, back propagation resolves the exploding or vanishing gradients difficulty in training traditional multi-layer neural networks with many layers. ReLU is the abbreviation of rectified linear unit, which applies the non-saturating activation functionf(x)=max(0,x). It successfully removes negative values from an activation map by setting them to zero. The nonlinear properties of the overall network and the decision function without affecting the receptive fields of the convolution layer are increased by it. Other functions are also used to extend nonlinearity, for instance the saturating hyperbolic tangent f(x)=tanh(x), f(x)=|tanh(x)| and the sigmoid function sigma(x)=(1+e^- x)^-1 . Since it trains the neural network several times faster without a large kr significant penalty to generalization accuracy, ReLU is preferred a lot more than the other functions.

5. Graphical User Interface The final part of the project includes a graphic user interface(GUI) which will act as a platform to feed fresh cell images for the module to detect whether the given image is cancerous or non cancerous. For this we use Flask. Flask is a web application framework which is written in python. It means by using flask,with the help of the tools, libraries and technologies provided by it , a complete web application can be built. This specific web application can be anything from wiki, a web page, a blog to something as big as a commercial website or a webbased major application. Flask also supports extensions that can add application details and characteristics as if they were implemented in Flask . It has proven to be a significant tool for learning web development basics and best techniques along with the main elements of a web International Research Journal of Engineering and Technology framework that are regular to almost all frameworks. Using all these components a GUI is created which will help in the classification of a new image.

GUI 5. MODEL IMPLEMENTATION Neural Network algorithm has been applied on the dataset in this stage. Neural network here works like a human biological method. In which we have to provide the input and get the output. But in these two layers, some hidden layers are present and it becomes mandatory that some additional process must be added before calculating the final output. These added units of bias, some of additional hidden layers, calculate the activation function and the final output is generated. The following parameters for calculating and training the model have been used in this model. Fig -4: Neural Network Functionality Fig shows the basic functionality of the neural network in which after the fixed position the neurons are fired that is called threshold condition. Table -1: Parameters in CCN model Parameters used in CCN model Number of inputs 512 Number of neurons 512 Activation function Relu Number of epochs 10 6. RESULTS AND DISCUSSION In this paper we have proposed a Deep Learning with Neural Network algorithm for diagnosis and detection of breast cancer. For pre-processing breast cancer dataset , we have used the standardization method . Then we have implemented a neural network algorithm and achieved 87.64% accuracy. By using breast-histopathology-images we tested 1728 images and received 87.64% which shows promising results as compared to other machine learning algorithms. Fig -5: Result of model 7. CONCLUSIONS

Cancer detection using machine learning is a system that mainly targets the early detection of cancer. With the ever increasing surge in the number of cancer diagnosis there is a need for better technology that increases the chance of survival. Hence we aim to use machine learning for early diagnosis which eventually increases the survival rate. For this, we have fed the machine with categorized data sets of malignant and benign cell images and for better results we have also shuffled these images within themselves and then have successfully trained the machine with malignant and benign data sets after which successful testing is performed with an unknown data set.

Breast cancer is one of the major causes of death in women around the world. According to the American cancer society, 41,760 women and more than 500 men died from breast cancer recently1. Breast cancer occurs in four main types: normal, benign, in-situ carcinoma and invasive carcinoma [. A benign tumor involves a minor change in the breast structure. It is not harmful and does not classify as a harmful cancer. In cases of in-situ carcinoma, the cancer is only in the mammary duct lobule system and does not affect other organs. This type is not dangerous and can be treated if diagnosed early. Invasive carcinoma is considered to be the most dangerous type of breast cancer, as it can spread to all other organs. According to the authors in [1], breast cancer can be detected using several methods including X-ray mammography, ultrasound (US), Computed Tomography (CT), Portion Emission Tomography (PET), Magnetic Resonance Imaging (MRI) and breast temperature measurement. Usually, the golden standard is a pathological diagnosis for detecting breast cancer. This involves an image analysis of the removed tissue, which is stained in the lab to increase visibility. Hematoxylin and Eosin (H&E) are commonly used for the staining process. Breast cancer can be diagnosed using one of two approaches: histopathological image analysis or genomics. Histopathological images are microscopic images of breast tissue that are extremely useful in early treatment of the cancer. As for genomics, the authors in stated that radio1 https://www.cancer.org/ Artificial Intelligence in Medicine, Elsevier, Vol 127, May 2022 genomics is an emerging research field focusing on multi-scale associations between medical imaging and gene expression data. Radio-genomics provide both radiological and genetic features that can enhance diagnosis. It can analyze tissues at the molecular level, helping with prediction and early detection of cancer. The main difference between imaging information and radio-genomics is the critical knowledge gap between imaging at the tissue level and analyzing the underlying molecular and genetic disease biomarkers. As imaging is less precise, it may lead to over- or under-treatment. While radio-genomics is much more effective than histopathological imaging, it is rarely used because the process involves datasets that are very expensive and require high computational power. As a result, a limited number of labs conduct radio-genomics experiments [.

This research paper addresses the following research questions and highlights the deep learning models, looking at their performance, the datasets used and possibilities for breast cancer classification and detection. 1. Which deep learning models perform most effectively? We will compare deep learning models with classical machine learning models to compare their performance. We will also list the performance metrics used. 2. What are the most used features for breast cancer classification? How are these features selected and extracted? We will observe the most important features that contribute to breast cancer classification, and the methods used to extract these features. 3. What datasets are available for both gene sequencing and MRI? What feature selection and extraction methods are

used? We will list and discuss all public and private datasets for gene sequencing and MRI imaging data. We will also list some of the methods used to select and extract the features. 4. Comparing gene sequence data with image data, for breast cancer detection problem, what are the drawbacks, challenges, and advantages? We will compare imaging and gene sequencing as they relate to breast cancer detection, using a tabular presentation to highlight the main differences between the two approaches. This is structured as follows:

Section 2 presents related work which includes surveys conducted in breast cancer area.

Section 3 explains the methodology used to conduct this research.

Section 4 presents the obtained results and related discussions.

Lastly, Section 5 concludes the paper and suggests future research directions. 2. Related Work Many studies have been conducted about breast cancer detection through imaging or through genomics. However, to the best of our knowledge, no research has been conducted including both techniques. The authors in [1] summarized the various techniques used to classify breast cancer using histopathological image analysis (HIA) based on different architectures of Artificial Neural Networks (ANN). The authors Artificial Intelligence in Medicine, Elsevier, Vol 127, May 2022 grouped their work according to the applied dataset. They arranged it in ascending chronological order. This work found that ANNs were first used in the field of HIA around 2012. ANNs and PNNs were the most frequently applied algorithms. However, in feature extraction, most of the work used textural and morphological features. It was clear that Deep CNNs were quite effective for early detection and diagnosis of breast cancer, leading to more successful treatment. Prediction of Non-Communicable Diseases (NCDs) was conducted using many algorithms.

In this the authors compared the performance of various classification algorithms. The classification algorithms were performed on eight NCD datasets using eight classification algorithms and a 10-fold crossvalidation method. These were evaluated using AUC as an indicator of accuracy. The authors stated that the NCD datasets have noisy data and irrelevant attributes. KNN, SVM and NN proved to be robust to this noise. In addition, they stated that the irrelevant attribute problem can be handled with some pre-processing techniques to improve the accuracy rate. Natural inspired computing (NIC) algorithms have been designed and applied to diagnose various human disorders. The authors in [3)introduced five insect-based NIC algorithms used for diagnosing diabetes and cancer. The authors found that it achieved a high level of performance in detecting different types of cancer (breast, lung, prostate and ovarian). To be more specific, breast cancer was detected using a hybridization of the guided ABC and neural networks. The authors also developed a highly effective methodology of detecting diabetes and leukemia. They concluded that the hybridization of NICs with other classification algorithms produces more precise and promising results. They mentioned that more work is required to detect different stages of diabetes and cancer.

In [4], the authors demonstrated the effectiveness of NNs in the classification of cancer diagnoses, especially in the initial stages. According to their study, the majority of NNs have shown promise in detecting tumor cells. However, the imaging approach requires high computational capacity to preprocess the images.

In [5], the authors reviewed different machine learning, deep learning and data mining algorithms related to breast cancer prediction. Several research papers on breast cancer were reviewed, with a total of 27 papers in machine learning, 4 papers in ensemble techniques and 8 papers in deep learning techniques. The authors mentioned that most of the papers used imaging, while only a few papers used genetics. The main algorithms used to predict breast cancer using genetics were SVM, decision tree and random forest. However, imaging techniques used several algorithms such as CNNs and Naïve Bayes. On the other hand, the authors

in [6] focused on gene mutation for detecting breast cancer. They mentioned that the gene prediction classification phase aims to carry out gene annotation, gene finding and gene mutation detection to ascertain the presence or absence of a cancer. They concluded that several methods can be used including regression, probability models, SVMs, NNs and deep learning. They also mentioned the many opportunities available to capture the relationship between nucleotide and feature extraction, since DNA sequencing involves a large amount of data in the form of a string sequence.

In [7], the authors examined recent studies applying deep learning to breast cancer with different imaging modalities. They organized these studies using the aspects of dataset, architecture, application and evaluation. They focused on deep learning frameworks developed in three breast imaging modalities (ultrasound, mammography and MRI). In their work, they attempted to provide state-of-the-art findings about breast cancer imaging utilizing DLR-based CAD systems. Their study included private datasets and classification using CNNs. Artificial Intelligence in Medicine, Elsevier, Vol 127, May 2022

After studying these surveys, our contribution will involve studying genetic sequencing and imaging at the same time to predict breast cancer and to get more information that can help early diagnosis and treatment of breast cancer. We will also provide recommendations to researchers who wish to conduct research in this area. 3. Methodology Our target topic is breast cancer detection using deep learning. We ended up using around 80 of the most recent papers related to breast cancer treatment and diagnosis. Some of the papers examined only deep learning, while others used a combination of machine learning and deep learning. In our search process, we mainly used the Scopus database to obtain the articles. This is to exclude nonrefereed publications However, in Figure 1, we state the distribution of selected papers among the existing databases. The top five databases are PubMed, ScienceDirect (Elsevier), IEEE, Springer and Nature.

The imaging modalities we considered were ultrasound, radiography, mammography and magnetic resonance imaging (MRI), as well as various types of gene expression and gene sequencing. In this research, we focused on papers that implement the breast cancer detection using the techniques of AI, as well as papers that predict breast cancer using both gene data and image data. We applied the following eligibility criteria on each paper: (1) The language is English; (2) The topic is related to breast cancer detection and treatment; (3) The paper discusses hybrid models of machine learning and deep learning; (4) The paper purely discusses deep learning; (5) The paper discusses genetic expression data; (6) The paper discusses imaging data; (7) Only journal and conference publications are retained; (8) Only medical or biomedical engineering publications are kept which are related to the topic. Please

note that non-refereed publications were excluded from the study. Firstly, we recorded the main information such as the name of the paper, year of publication, the list of authors and the publisher. Then, we included some information to conduct the systematic review, such as the algorithm used and whether the paper discusses only deep learning or a hybrid between DL and ML, the recorded accuracy and other performance evaluation parameters, the dataset, the features, and many other columns. We answered our research questions using these criteria. 4. Results and Discussion In this systematic study, our initial search turned up 1,000 conference and journal papers. After eliminating duplicated papers and unrelated studies that were "purely medical or about cancer in general", we ended up with 80 papers related to both ML and DL.

In machine learning method, data and output is run on the computer to create a program :

1. Sparse compact incremental learning machine (SCILM) method A new approach was designed to resolve cancer classification problem on microarray gene expression data, which take advantage of correntropy cost that makes it robust against diverse noises and outliers. Moreover, since SCILM uses l1-norm of the weights, it has sparseness, which can be applied for gene selection purposes as well. Finally, due to compact structure, the method is capable of performing classification tasks in all of the cases with only one neuron in its hidden layer. The experimental analysis in this method was performed on 26 well-known microarray data sets regarding diverse kinds of cancers and the results showed that the strategy not only achieved significantly high accuracy but also accompanied with effectivity of each gene regarding the corresponding cancer .

2. Knowledge base system learning method A new knowledge-based system for classification of cancer disease was proposed using clustering, noise removal, and classification techniques. Expectation Maximization (EM) was used as a clustering method to cluster the data in similar groups. Classification and Regression Trees (CART) were used to generate the fuzzy rules to be used for the classification of cancer disease in the knowledge-based system of fuzzy rule-based reasoning method. To overcome the multicollinearity issue, Principal Component Analysis (PCA) was incorporated in the current knowledge-based system. Experimental results on Wisconsin Diagnostic Breast Cancer and Mammographic mass datasets showed that current approach remarkably improves the prediction accuracy of breast cancer. The knowledge-based system can be used .

3. Gauss-Newton representation based learning method A novel Gauss-Newton representation based algorithm (GNRBA) for breast cancer classification. It uses the sparse representation with training sample selection. Until now, sparse representation has been successfully applied in pattern recognition only. This method introduces a novel Gauss-Newton based approach to find the optimal weights for the training samples for classification. In addition, it evaluates the sparsity in a computationally efficient way as compared to the conventional l1-norm method. The effectiveness of the GNRBA is examined on the Wisconsin Breast Cancer Database (WBCD) and the Wisconsin Diagnosis Breast Cancer (WDBC) database from the UCI Machine Learning repository. Various performance measures like classification accuracy, sensitivity, specificity, confusion matrices, a statistical test and the area under the receiver operating characteristic (AUC) are reported to show the superiority of the proposed method as compared to classical models [17].

4. Gene expression learning method Studying the characteristics of thousands of genes simultaneously offered a deep insight into cancer classification problem. It introduced an abundant amount of data ready to be explored. It has also been applied in a wide range of applications such as drug discovery, cancer prediction and diagnosis which is a very important issue for cancer treatment . Besides, it helps in understanding the function of genes and the interaction between genes in

normal and abnormal conditions . That is done by monitoring the behavior of genes, gene expression data under different conditions. Ensemble classifiers increase not only the performance of the classification, but also the confidence of the results. The motivations beyond using ensemble classifiers are that the results are less dependent on peculiarities of a single training set and because the ensemble system outperforms the performance of the best base classifier in the ensemble [19].

5. Ensemble predictive modeling framework learning method Molecular changes often precede clinical presentation of diseases and can be useful surrogates with potential to assist in informed clinical decision making. Recent studies have demonstrated the usefulness of modeling approaches such as classification that can predict the clinical outcomes from molecular expression profiles. While useful, a majority of these approaches implicitly use all molecular markers as features in the classification process often resulting in sparse high-dimensional projection of the samples often comparable to that of the sample size. Ensemble classification approach is used for predicting good and poorprognosis breast cancer samples from their molecular expression profiles [20]. In contrast to traditional single and ensemble classifiers, the proposed approach uses multiple base classifiers with varying feature sets obtained from two-dimensional projection of the samples in conjunction with a majority voting strategy for predicting the class labels .

In contrast to earlier implementation, base classifiers in the ensembles are chosen based on maximal sensitivity and minimal redundancy by choosing only those with low average cosine distance. The resulting ensemble sets are subsequently modeled as undirected graphs. Performance of four different classification algorithms is shown to be better within the proposed ensemble framework in contrast to using them as traditional single classifier systems. Design of an efficient ensemble predictive modeling classification framework for prediction of breast density class .

6. Convolution neural network learning method Deep convolutional neural networks (CNNs) were designed to obtain more discriminative description of cancer tissues. Benefiting from the discriminative representation, metric learning layers are proposed to further improve performance of the deep structure. The bestperforming model restricts the depth of back I J Mutil Re App St Volume 1 Issue 1, 2017 PP. 1-8 6|Page propagation of joint training in only the metric learning layers. Relation between metric learning layers and tradition CNNs structures seems like parasitism relationship between species, where one species, the parasite, benefits at the expense of the other . Therefore, the method is named as parasitic metric learning net. To confirm veracity of this method, classification experiments on breast mass images of two widely used databases were performed . Comparing performance of the current method with traditional ones, competitive results were achieved. Meanwhile, the parameter updating strategy for parasitic metric net may inspire a way of improving performance of a pre-trained CNNs model on

particular medical image processing or other computer vision tasks . Training pipeline of the proposed parasitic metric learning net .We discussed the concepts of machine learning while we outlined their application in cancer prediction/prognosis. Most of the studies that have been proposed the last years and focus on the development of predictive models using supervised machine learning methods and classification algorithms aiming to predict valid disease outcomes. Based on the analysis of their results, it is evident that the integration of multidimensional heterogeneous data, combined with the application of different techniques for feature selection and classification can provide promising tools for inference in the cancer domain.

EXPERIMENT AND METHODOLOGY :.

1 Data-sets A malignant tumour that has developed from cells of the breast is breast cancer. Although some of the scientifically known risk factors (i.e. ageing, genetic risk factors, family history, menstrual periods, not having children, obesity) that increase a woman's chance of developing breast cancer, the exact causes or some of these risk factors that causes cells to become cancerous are not exactly known by them. Research is under way to learn more and scientists are making great progress in understanding how certain changes in DNA can cause normal breast cells to become cancerous. This part of the project includes the research about the available dataset that can be used for the project. The initial dataset that we planned on working had certain drawbacks. CBIS-DDSM dataset: Neither the analytics nor the experimental validation of the data were sufficient to move forward with the project. There was no exact data regarding the classification of tumours into benign and malignant in case of scan images of patients. One the most important demerit of this dataset was the improper organization of data and huge redundant records which can cause glitches in the training process. Hence it was concluded that evaluation based on detection rate and accuracy levels with this data-set is not appropriate. Breast cancer Wisconsin data-set: This dataset was a text type data-set which had a classified set of data into malignant and benign tumours based on the cell features threshold values for various features like cell radius, perimeter, area, symmetry and other such International Research Journal of Engineering and Technology . We didn't go for this data-set since we planned on a better version of cancer detection model which focused on images

2 Pre-processing data Data preprocessing is a data mining technique that is used for filter data in a usable format. Because the real-world data-set is almost available in different formats. It's not available as per our requirement so it must fit the data-set in an understandable format. Data pre processing is a proven method of resolving such issues. Data pre-processing converts the data-set into usable format for pre-processing. We have used a standardization method to pre- process the data-set. Encoder Method: Label Encoder is an efficient tool for encoding the levels of the categorical features into numeric values. Label Encoder encode labels with value between 0 and classes -1. All our categorical features are encoded. In this paper we have classified malignant and Benign in diagnosis with 0 and 1. After encoding the dataset we have applied a neural network on these dataset and achieved accuracy.

3 Normalizer Method Normalization is a better technique to use when distribution of the data is unknown.. Data normalization is the process of rescaling one and more attributes to the range of 0 to 1. This means that the largest value for each attribute is 1 and the smallest value is 0. After applying the Label Encoder method all dataset

is converted into numeric dataset. Because Label Encoder encodes all string label dataset into numeric dataset. Normalization process is known to work on numeric dataset. So after normalized data we have applied a neural network on that dataset and achieved accuracy. But again accuracy is not yet adequate. So we have applied the next process for pre-processing.

.4. Convolutional Neural Network Convolutional Neural Network is a type of neural network technique which has proven to be specifically efficient with image recognition and classification. The input is a tensor with shape (number of images) x (image width) x (image height) x (image depth) in the programming CNN. Then the image becomes abstracted to a feature map, with shape (number of images) x (feature map width) x (feature map height) x (feature map channels)after passing through a convolutional layer. The following attributes are expected in a convolutional layer within a neural network : • Width and height (hyper-parameters) defined by convolutional kernels. • The number of input channels and output channels (hyper-parameter). • The number channels (depth) of the input feature map must be equal to depth of the Convolution filter (the input channels) The convolution of input and passing its result to the next layer is done by Convolutional layers. This is similar to the response of a neuron in the visual cortex to a specific stimulus. Each and every convolutional neuron processes data only for its receptive field. It is not practical to apply this architecture to images, even though fully connected feed forward neural networks can be used to learn features as well as classify data. Due to the very large input sizes related with images, a very high number of neurons would be required, even in a simplistic architecture which is not very deep, where each pixel is a relevant variable. For example,in the second layer, a fully connected layer for an image of size 100 x 100 has 10,000 weights for each neuron. A way out to this issue is provided by the convolution operation by decreasing the number of free parameters, allowing the network to be even deeper with keeping the parameters few. Taking an example, irrespective of image size, tiling regions of size 5 x 5, each with the same shared weights, requires only 25 learnable parameters. If went by this, back propagation resolves the exploding or vanishing gradients difficulty in training traditional multi-layer neural networks with many layers. ReLU is the abbreviation of rectified linear unit, which applies the non-saturating activation functionf(x)=max(0,x). It successfully removes negative values from an activation map by setting them to zero. The nonlinear properties of the overall network and the decision function without affecting the receptive fields of the convolution layer are increased by it. Other functions are also used to extend nonlinearity, for instance the saturating hyperbolic tangent f(x)=tanh(x), f(x)=|tanh(x)| and the sigmoid function sigma(x)=(1+e^- x)^-1 . Since it trains the neural network several times faster without a large kr significant penalty to generalization accuracy, ReLU is preferred a lot more than the other functions.

5. Graphical User Interface The final part of the project includes a graphic user interface(GUI) which will act as a platform to feed fresh cell images for the module to detect whether the given image is cancerous or non cancerous. For this we use Flask. Flask is a web application framework which is written in python. It means by using flask,with the help of the tools, libraries and technologies provided by it , a complete web application can be built. This specific web application can be anything from wiki, a web page, a blog to something as big as a commercial website or a webbased major application. Flask also supports extensions that can add application details and characteristics as if

they were implemented in Flask . It has proven to be a significant tool for learning web development basics and best techniques along with the main elements of a web International Research Journal of Engineering and Technology framework that are regular to almost all frameworks. Using all these components a GUI is created which will help in the classification of a new image.

GUI 5. MODEL IMPLEMENTATION Neural Network algorithm has been applied on the dataset in this stage. Neural network here works like a human biological method. In which we have to provide the input and get the output. But in these two layers, some hidden layers are present and it becomes mandatory that some additional process must be added before calculating the final output. These added units of bias, some of additional hidden layers, calculate the activation function and the final output is generated. The following parameters for calculating and training the model have been used in this model. Fig -4: Neural Network Functionality Fig shows the basic functionality of the neural network in which after the fixed position the neurons are fired that is called threshold condition. Table -1: Parameters in CCN model Parameters used in CCN model Number of inputs 512 Number of neurons 512 Activation function Relu Number of epochs 10 6. RESULTS AND DISCUSSION In this paper we have proposed a Deep Learning with Neural Network algorithm for diagnosis and detection of breast cancer. For pre-processing breast cancer dataset , we have used the standardization method . Then we have implemented a neural network algorithm and achieved 87.64% accuracy. By using breast-histopathology-images we tested 1728 images and received 87.64% which shows promising results as compared to other machine learning algorithms. Fig -5: Result of model 7. CONCLUSIONS Cancer detection using machine learning is a system that mainly targets the early detection of cancer. With the ever increasing surge in the number of cancer diagnosis there is a need for better technology that increases the chance of survival. Hence we aim to use machine learning for early diagnosis which eventually increases the survival rate. For this, we have fed the machine with categorized data sets of malignant and benign cell images and for better results we have also shuffled these images within themselves and then have successfully trained the machine with malignant and benign data sets after which successful testing is performed with an unknown data set.

Breast cancer is one of the major causes of death in women around the world. According to the American cancer society, 41,760 women and more than 500 men died from breast cancer recently1. Breast cancer occurs in four main types: normal, benign, in-situ carcinoma and invasive carcinoma [. A benign tumor involves a minor change in the breast structure. It is not harmful and does not classify as a harmful cancer. In cases of in-situ carcinoma, the cancer is only in the mammary duct lobule system and does not affect other organs. This type is not dangerous and can be treated if diagnosed early. Invasive carcinoma is considered to be the most dangerous type of breast cancer, as it can spread to all other organs. According to the authors in [1], breast cancer can be detected using several methods including X-ray mammography, ultrasound (US), Computed Tomography (CT), Portion Emission Tomography (PET), Magnetic Resonance Imaging (MRI) and breast temperature measurement. Usually, the golden standard is a pathological diagnosis for detecting breast cancer. This involves an image analysis of the removed tissue, which is stained in the lab to increase visibility. Hematoxylin and Eosin (H&E) are commonly used for the staining process. Breast cancer can be diagnosed using one of two approaches: histopathological image analysis or genomics.

Histopathological images are microscopic images of breast tissue that are extremely useful in early treatment of the cancer. As for genomics, the authors in stated that radio1 https://www.cancer.org/ Artificial Intelligence in Medicine, Elsevier, Vol 127, May 2022 genomics is an emerging research field focusing on multi-scale associations between medical imaging and gene expression data. Radio-genomics provide both radiological and genetic features that can enhance diagnosis. It can analyze tissues at the molecular level, helping with prediction and early detection of cancer. The main difference between imaging information and radio-genomics is the critical knowledge gap between imaging at the tissue level and analyzing the underlying molecular and genetic disease biomarkers. As imaging is less precise, it may lead to over- or under-treatment. While radio-genomics is much more effective than histopathological imaging, it is rarely used because the process involves datasets that are very expensive and require high computational power. As a result, a limited number of labs conduct radio-genomics experiments [.

This research paper addresses the following research questions and highlights the deep learning models, looking at their performance, the datasets used and possibilities for breast cancer classification and detection. 1. Which deep learning models perform most effectively? We will compare deep learning models with classical machine learning models to compare their performance. We will also list the performance metrics used. 2. What are the most used features for breast cancer classification? How are these features selected and extracted? We will observe the most important features that contribute to breast cancer classification, and the methods used to extract these features. 3. What datasets are available for both gene sequencing and MRI? What feature selection and extraction methods are used? We will list and discuss all public and private datasets for gene sequencing and MRI imaging data. We will also list some of the methods used to select and extract the features. 4. Comparing gene sequence data with image data, for breast cancer detection problem, what are the drawbacks, challenges, and advantages? We will compare imaging and gene sequencing as they relate to breast cancer detection, using a tabular presentation to highlight the main differences between the two approaches. This is structured as follows:

Section 2 presents related work which includes surveys conducted in breast cancer area.

Section 3 explains the methodology used to conduct this research.

Section 4 presents the obtained results and related discussions.

Lastly, Section 5 concludes the paper and suggests future research directions. 2. Related Work Many studies have been conducted about breast cancer detection through imaging or through genomics. However, to the best of our knowledge, no research has been conducted including both techniques. The authors in [1] summarized the various techniques used to classify breast cancer using histopathological image analysis (HIA) based on different architectures of Artificial Neural Networks (ANN). The authors Artificial Intelligence in Medicine, Elsevier, Vol 127, May 2022 grouped their work according to the applied dataset. They arranged it in ascending chronological order. This work found that ANNs were first used in the field of HIA around 2012. ANNs and PNNs were the most frequently applied algorithms. However, in feature extraction, most of the work used textural and morphological features. It was clear that Deep CNNs were quite effective for early detection and diagnosis of breast cancer, leading to more successful treatment. Prediction of Non-Communicable Diseases (NCDs) was conducted using many algorithms.

In this the authors compared the performance of various classification algorithms. The classification algorithms were performed on eight NCD datasets using eight classification algorithms and a 10-fold crossvalidation method. These were evaluated using AUC as an indicator of accuracy. The authors stated that the NCD datasets have noisy data and irrelevant attributes. KNN, SVM and NN proved to be robust to this noise. In addition, they stated that the irrelevant attribute problem can be handled with some pre-processing techniques to improve the accuracy rate. Natural inspired computing (NIC) algorithms have been designed and applied to diagnose various human disorders. The authors in [3)introduced five insect-based NIC algorithms used for diagnosing diabetes and cancer. The authors found that it achieved a high level of performance in detecting different types of cancer (breast, lung, prostate and ovarian). To be more specific, breast cancer was detected using a hybridization of the guided ABC and neural networks. The authors also developed a highly effective methodology of detecting diabetes and leukemia. They concluded that the hybridization of NICs with other classification algorithms produces more precise and promising results. They mentioned that more work is required to detect different stages of diabetes and cancer.

In [4], the authors demonstrated the effectiveness of NNs in the classification of cancer diagnoses, especially in the initial stages. According to their study, the majority of NNs have shown promise in detecting tumor cells. However, the imaging approach requires high computational capacity to preprocess the images.

In [5], the authors reviewed different machine learning, deep learning and data mining algorithms related to breast cancer prediction. Several research papers on breast cancer were reviewed, with a total of 27 papers in machine learning, 4 papers in ensemble techniques and 8 papers in deep learning techniques. The authors mentioned that most of the papers used imaging, while only a few papers used genetics. The main algorithms used to predict breast cancer using genetics were SVM, decision tree and random forest. However, imaging techniques used several algorithms such as CNNs and Naïve Bayes. On the other hand, the authors

in [6] focused on gene mutation for detecting breast cancer. They mentioned that the gene prediction classification phase aims to carry out gene annotation, gene finding and gene mutation detection to ascertain the presence or absence of a cancer. They concluded that several methods can be used including regression, probability models, SVMs, NNs and deep learning. They also mentioned the many opportunities available to capture the relationship between nucleotide and feature extraction, since DNA sequencing involves a large amount of data in the form of a string sequence.

In [7], the authors examined recent studies applying deep learning to breast cancer with different imaging modalities. They organized these studies using the aspects of dataset, architecture, application and evaluation. They focused on deep learning frameworks developed in three breast imaging modalities (ultrasound, mammography and MRI). In their work, they attempted to provide state-of-the-art findings about breast cancer imaging utilizing DLR-based CAD systems. Their study included private datasets and classification using CNNs. Artificial Intelligence in Medicine, Elsevier, Vol 127, May 2022

After studying these surveys, our contribution will involve studying genetic sequencing and imaging at the same time to predict breast cancer and to get more information that can help early diagnosis and treatment of breast cancer. We will also provide recommendations to researchers who wish to conduct research in this area. 3. Methodology Our target topic is breast cancer detection using deep learning. We ended up using around 80 of the most recent papers related to breast cancer treatment and diagnosis. Some of the papers examined only deep learning, while others used a combination of machine learning and deep learning. In our search process, we mainly used the Scopus database to obtain the articles. This is to exclude nonrefereed publications However, in Figure 1, we state the distribution of selected papers among the existing databases. The top five databases are PubMed, ScienceDirect (Elsevier), IEEE, Springer and Nature.

The imaging modalities we considered were ultrasound, radiography, mammography and magnetic resonance imaging (MRI), as well as various types of gene expression and gene sequencing. In this research, we focused on papers that implement the breast cancer detection using the techniques of AI, as well as papers that predict breast cancer using both gene data and image data. We applied the following eligibility criteria on each paper: (1) The language is English; (2) The topic is related to breast cancer detection and treatment; (3) The paper discusses hybrid models of machine learning and deep learning; (4) The paper purely discusses deep learning; (5) The paper discusses genetic expression data; (6) The paper discusses imaging data; (7) Only journal and conference publications are retained; (8) Only medical or biomedical engineering publications are kept which are related to the topic. Please note that non-refereed publications were excluded from the study. Firstly, we recorded the main information such as the name of the paper, year of publication, the list of authors and the publisher. Then, we included some information to conduct the systematic review, such as the algorithm used and whether the paper discusses only deep learning or a hybrid between DL and ML, the recorded accuracy and other performance evaluation parameters, the dataset, the features, and many other columns. We answered our research questions using these criteria. 4. Results and Discussion In this systematic study, our initial search turned up 1,000 conference and journal papers. After eliminating duplicated papers and unrelated studies that were "purely medical or about cancer in general", we ended up with 80 papers related to both ML and DL.

In machine learning method, data and output is run on the computer to create a program :

1. Sparse compact incremental learning machine (SCILM) method A new approach was designed to resolve cancer classification problem on microarray gene expression data, which take advantage of correntropy cost that makes it robust against diverse noises and outliers. Moreover, since SCILM uses l1-norm of the weights, it has sparseness, which can be applied for gene selection purposes as well. Finally, due to compact structure, the method is capable of performing classification tasks in all of the cases with only one neuron in its hidden layer. The experimental analysis in this method was performed on 26 well-known microarray data sets regarding diverse kinds of cancers and the results showed that the strategy not only achieved significantly high accuracy but also accompanied with effectivity of each gene regarding the corresponding cancer .

2. Knowledge base system learning method A new knowledge-based system for classification of cancer disease was proposed using clustering, noise removal, and classification techniques. Expectation Maximization (EM) was used as a clustering method to cluster the data in similar groups. Classification and Regression Trees (CART) were used to generate the fuzzy rules to be used for the classification of cancer disease in the knowledge-based system of fuzzy rule-based reasoning method. To overcome the multicollinearity issue, Principal Component Analysis (PCA) was incorporated in the current knowledge-based system. Experimental results on Wisconsin Diagnostic Breast Cancer and Mammographic mass datasets showed that current approach remarkably improves the prediction accuracy of breast cancer. The knowledge-based system can be used .

3. Gauss-Newton representation based learning method A novel Gauss-Newton representation based algorithm (GNRBA) for breast cancer classification. It uses the sparse representation with training sample selection. Until now, sparse representation has been successfully applied in pattern recognition only. This method introduces a novel Gauss-Newton based approach to find the optimal weights for the training samples for classification. In addition, it evaluates the sparsity in a computationally efficient way as compared to the conventional l1-norm method. The effectiveness of the GNRBA is examined on the Wisconsin Breast Cancer Database (WBCD) and the Wisconsin Diagnosis Breast Cancer (WDBC) database from the UCI Machine Learning repository. Various performance measures like classification accuracy, sensitivity, specificity, confusion matrices, a statistical test and the area under the receiver operating characteristic (AUC) are reported to show the superiority of the proposed method as compared to classical models [17].

4. Gene expression learning method Studying the characteristics of thousands of genes simultaneously offered a deep insight into cancer classification problem. It introduced an abundant amount of data ready to be explored. It has also been applied in a wide range of applications such as drug discovery, cancer prediction and diagnosis which is a very important issue for cancer treatment . Besides, it helps in understanding the function of genes and the interaction between genes in

normal and abnormal conditions . That is done by monitoring the behavior of genes, gene expression data under different conditions. Ensemble classifiers increase not only the performance of the classification, but also the confidence of the results. The motivations beyond using ensemble classifiers are that the results are less dependent on peculiarities of a single training set and because the ensemble system outperforms the performance of the best base classifier in the ensemble [19].

5. Ensemble predictive modeling framework learning method Molecular changes often precede clinical presentation of diseases and can be useful surrogates with potential to assist in informed clinical decision making. Recent studies have demonstrated the usefulness of modeling approaches such as classification that can predict the clinical outcomes from molecular expression profiles. While useful, a majority of these approaches implicitly use all molecular markers as features in the classification process often resulting in sparse high-dimensional projection of the samples often comparable to that of the sample size. Ensemble classification approach is used for predicting good and poorprognosis breast cancer samples from their molecular expression profiles [20]. In contrast to traditional

single and ensemble classifiers, the proposed approach uses multiple base classifiers with varying feature sets obtained from two-dimensional projection of the samples in conjunction with a majority voting strategy for predicting the class labels .

In contrast to earlier implementation, base classifiers in the ensembles are chosen based on maximal sensitivity and minimal redundancy by choosing only those with low average cosine distance. The resulting ensemble sets are subsequently modeled as undirected graphs. Performance of four different classification algorithms is shown to be better within the proposed ensemble framework in contrast to using them as traditional single classifier systems. Design of an efficient ensemble predictive modeling classification framework for prediction of breast density class .

6. Convolution neural network learning method Deep convolutional neural networks (CNNs) were designed to obtain more discriminative description of cancer tissues. Benefiting from the discriminative representation, metric learning layers are proposed to further improve performance of the deep structure. The bestperforming model restricts the depth of back I J Mutil Re App St Volume 1 Issue 1, 2017 PP. 1-8 6|Page propagation of joint training in only the metric learning layers. Relation between metric learning layers and tradition CNNs structures seems like parasitism relationship between species, where one species, the parasite, benefits at the expense of the other . Therefore, the method is named as parasitic metric learning net. To confirm veracity of this method, classification experiments on breast mass images of two widely used databases were performed . Comparing performance of the current method with traditional ones, competitive results were achieved. Meanwhile, the parameter updating strategy for parasitic metric net may inspire a way of improving performance of a pre-trained CNNs model on particular medical image processing or other computer vision tasks . Training pipeline of the proposed parasitic metric learning net .We discussed the concepts of machine learning while we outlined their application in cancer prediction/prognosis. Most of the studies that have been proposed the last years and focus on the development of predictive models using supervised machine learning methods and classification algorithms aiming to predict valid disease outcomes. Based on the analysis of their results, it is evident that the integration of multidimensional heterogeneous data, combined with the application of different techniques for feature selection and classification can provide promising tools for inference in the cancer domain.

EXPERIMENT AND METHODOLOGY :.

1 Data-sets A malignant tumour that has developed from cells of the breast is breast cancer. Although some of the scientifically known risk factors (i.e. ageing, genetic risk factors, family history, menstrual periods, not having children, obesity) that increase a woman's chance of developing breast cancer, the exact causes or some of these risk factors that causes cells to become cancerous are not exactly known by them. Research is under way to learn more and scientists are making great progress in understanding how certain changes in DNA can cause normal breast cells to become cancerous. This part of the project includes the research about the available dataset that can be used for the project. The initial dataset that we planned on working had certain drawbacks. CBIS-DDSM dataset: Neither the analytics nor the experimental validation of the data were sufficient to move forward with the project. There was no exact data regarding the classification of tumours into benign and malignant in case of scan images of patients.

One the most important demerit of this dataset was the improper organization of data and huge redundant records which can cause glitches in the training process. Hence it was concluded that evaluation based on detection rate and accuracy levels with this data-set is not appropriate. Breast cancer Wisconsin data-set: This dataset was a text type data-set which had a classified set of data into malignant and benign tumours based on the cell features threshold values for various features like cell radius, perimeter, area, symmetry and other such International Research Journal of Engineering and Technology . We didn't go for this data-set since we planned on a better version of cancer detection model which focused on images

2 Pre-processing data Data preprocessing is a data mining technique that is used for filter data in a usable format. Because the real-world data-set is almost available in different formats. It's not available as per our requirement so it must fit the data-set in an understandable format. Data pre processing is a proven method of resolving such issues. Data pre-processing converts the data-set into usable format for pre-processing. We have used a standardization method to pre- process the data-set. Encoder Method: Label Encoder is an efficient tool for encoding the levels of the categorical features into numeric values. Label Encoder encode labels with value between 0 and classes -1. All our categorical features are encoded. In this paper we have classified malignant and Benign in diagnosis with 0 and 1. After encoding the dataset we have applied a neural network on these dataset and achieved accuracy.

3 Normalizer Method Normalization is a better technique to use when distribution of the data is unknown.. Data normalization is the process of rescaling one and more attributes to the range of 0 to 1. This means that the largest value for each attribute is 1 and the smallest value is 0. After applying the Label Encoder method all dataset is converted into numeric dataset. Because Label Encoder encodes all string label dataset into numeric dataset. Normalization process is known to work on numeric dataset. So after normalized data we have applied a neural network on that dataset and achieved accuracy. But again accuracy is not yet adequate. So we have applied the next process for pre-processing.

.4. Convolutional Neural Network Convolutional Neural Network is a type of neural network technique which has proven to be specifically efficient with image recognition and classification. The input is a tensor with shape (number of images) x (image width) x (image height) x (image depth) in the programming CNN. Then the image becomes abstracted to a feature map, with shape (number of images) x (feature map width) x (feature map height) x (feature map channels)after passing through a convolutional layer. The following attributes are expected in a convolutional layer within a neural network : • Width and height (hyper-parameters) defined by convolutional kernels. • The number of input channels and output channels (hyper-parameter). • The number channels (depth) of the input feature map must be equal to depth of the Convolution filter (the input channels) The convolution of input and passing its result to the next layer is done by Convolutional layers. This is similar to the response of a neuron in the visual cortex to a specific stimulus. Each and every convolutional neuron processes data only for its receptive field. It is not practical to apply this architecture to images, even though fully connected feed forward neural networks can be used to learn features as well as classify data. Due to the very large input sizes related with images, a very high number of neurons would be required, even in a simplistic architecture which is not very deep, where each

pixel is a relevant variable. For example,in the second layer, a fully connected layer for an image of size 100 x 100 has 10,000 weights for each neuron. A way out to this issue is provided by the convolution operation by decreasing the number of free parameters, allowing the network to be even deeper with keeping the parameters few. Taking an example, irrespective of image size, tiling regions of size 5 x 5, each with the same shared weights, requires only 25 learnable parameters. If went by this, back propagation resolves the exploding or vanishing gradients difficulty in training traditional multi-layer neural networks with many layers. ReLU is the abbreviation of rectified linear unit, which applies the non-saturating activation functionf(x)=max(0,x). It successfully removes negative values from an activation map by setting them to zero. The nonlinear properties of the overall network and the decision function without affecting the receptive fields of the convolution layer are increased by it. Other functions are also used to extend nonlinearity, for instance the saturating hyperbolic tangent f(x)=tanh(x), f(x)= | tanh(x) | and the sigmoid function sigma(x)=(1+e^- x)^-1 . Since it trains the neural network several times faster without a large kr significant penalty to generalization accuracy, ReLU is preferred a lot more than the other functions.

5. Graphical User Interface The final part of the project includes a graphic user interface(GUI) which will act as a platform to feed fresh cell images for the module to detect whether the given image is cancerous or non cancerous. For this we use Flask. Flask is a web application framework which is written in python. It means by using flask,with the help of the tools, libraries and technologies provided by it , a complete web application can be built. This specific web application can be anything from wiki, a web page, a blog to something as big as a commercial website or a webbased major application. Flask also supports extensions that can add application details and characteristics as if they were implemented in Flask . It has proven to be a significant tool for learning web development basics and best techniques along with the main elements of a web International Research Journal of Engineering and Technology framework that are regular to almost all frameworks. Using all these components a GUI is created which will help in the classification of a new image.

GUI 5. MODEL IMPLEMENTATION Neural Network algorithm has been applied on the dataset in this stage. Neural network here works like a human biological method. In which we have to provide the input and get the output. But in these two layers, some hidden layers are present and it becomes mandatory that some additional process must be added before calculating the final output. These added units of bias, some of additional hidden layers, calculate the activation function and the final output is generated. The following parameters for calculating and training the model have been used in this model. Fig -4: Neural Network Functionality Fig shows the basic functionality of the neural network in which after the fixed position the neurons are fired that is called threshold condition. Table -1: Parameters in CCN model Parameters used in CCN model Number of inputs 512 Number of neurons 512 Activation function Relu Number of epochs 10 6. RESULTS AND DISCUSSION In this paper we have proposed a Deep Learning with Neural Network algorithm for diagnosis and detection of breast cancer. For pre-processing breast cancer dataset , we have used the standardization method . Then we have implemented a neural network algorithm and achieved 87.64% accuracy. By using breast-histopathology-images we tested 1728 images and received 87.64% which shows promising results as compared to other machine learning algorithms. Fig -5: Result of model 7. CONCLUSIONS

Cancer detection using machine learning is a system that mainly targets the early detection of cancer. With the ever increasing surge in the number of cancer diagnosis there is a need for better technology that increases the chance of survival. Hence we aim to use machine learning for early diagnosis which eventually increases the survival rate. For this, we have fed the machine with categorized data sets of malignant and benign cell images and for better results we have also shuffled these images within themselves and then have successfully trained the machine with malignant and benign data sets after which successful testing is performed with an unknown data set.

Breast cancer is one of the major causes of death in women around the world. According to the American cancer society, 41,760 women and more than 500 men died from breast cancer recently1. Breast cancer occurs in four main types: normal, benign, in-situ carcinoma and invasive carcinoma [. A benign tumor involves a minor change in the breast structure. It is not harmful and does not classify as a harmful cancer. In cases of in-situ carcinoma, the cancer is only in the mammary duct lobule system and does not affect other organs. This type is not dangerous and can be treated if diagnosed early. Invasive carcinoma is considered to be the most dangerous type of breast cancer, as it can spread to all other organs. According to the authors in [1], breast cancer can be detected using several methods including X-ray mammography, ultrasound (US), Computed Tomography (CT), Portion Emission Tomography (PET), Magnetic Resonance Imaging (MRI) and breast temperature measurement. Usually, the golden standard is a pathological diagnosis for detecting breast cancer. This involves an image analysis of the removed tissue, which is stained in the lab to increase visibility. Hematoxylin and Eosin (H&E) are commonly used for the staining process. Breast cancer can be diagnosed using one of two approaches: histopathological image analysis or genomics. Histopathological images are microscopic images of breast tissue that are extremely useful in early treatment of the cancer. As for genomics, the authors in stated that radio1 https://www.cancer.org/ Artificial Intelligence in Medicine, Elsevier, Vol 127, May 2022 genomics is an emerging research field focusing on multi-scale associations between medical imaging and gene expression data. Radio-genomics provide both radiological and genetic features that can enhance diagnosis. It can analyze tissues at the molecular level, helping with prediction and early detection of cancer. The main difference between imaging information and radio-genomics is the critical knowledge gap between imaging at the tissue level and analyzing the underlying molecular and genetic disease biomarkers. As imaging is less precise, it may lead to over- or under-treatment. While radio-genomics is much more effective than histopathological imaging, it is rarely used because the process involves datasets that are very expensive and require high computational power. As a result, a limited number of labs conduct radio-genomics experiments [.

This research paper addresses the following research questions and highlights the deep learning models, looking at their performance, the datasets used and possibilities for breast cancer classification and detection. 1. Which deep learning models perform most effectively? We will compare deep learning models with classical machine learning models to compare their performance. We will also list the performance metrics used. 2. What are the most used features for breast cancer classification? How are these features selected and extracted? We will observe the most important features that contribute to breast cancer classification, and the methods used to extract these features. 3. What datasets are available for both gene sequencing and MRI? What feature selection and extraction methods are

used? We will list and discuss all public and private datasets for gene sequencing and MRI imaging data. We will also list some of the methods used to select and extract the features. 4. Comparing gene sequence data with image data, for breast cancer detection problem, what are the drawbacks, challenges, and advantages? We will compare imaging and gene sequencing as they relate to breast cancer detection, using a tabular presentation to highlight the main differences between the two approaches. This is structured as follows:

Section 2 presents related work which includes surveys conducted in breast cancer area.

Section 3 explains the methodology used to conduct this research.

Section 4 presents the obtained results and related discussions.

Lastly, Section 5 concludes the paper and suggests future research directions. 2. Related Work Many studies have been conducted about breast cancer detection through imaging or through genomics. However, to the best of our knowledge, no research has been conducted including both techniques. The authors in [1] summarized the various techniques used to classify breast cancer using histopathological image analysis (HIA) based on different architectures of Artificial Neural Networks (ANN). The authors Artificial Intelligence in Medicine, Elsevier, Vol 127, May 2022 grouped their work according to the applied dataset. They arranged it in ascending chronological order. This work found that ANNs were first used in the field of HIA around 2012. ANNs and PNNs were the most frequently applied algorithms. However, in feature extraction, most of the work used textural and morphological features. It was clear that Deep CNNs were quite effective for early detection and diagnosis of breast cancer, leading to more successful treatment. Prediction of Non-Communicable Diseases (NCDs) was conducted using many algorithms.

In this the authors compared the performance of various classification algorithms. The classification algorithms were performed on eight NCD datasets using eight classification algorithms and a 10-fold crossvalidation method. These were evaluated using AUC as an indicator of accuracy. The authors stated that the NCD datasets have noisy data and irrelevant attributes. KNN, SVM and NN proved to be robust to this noise. In addition, they stated that the irrelevant attribute problem can be handled with some pre-processing techniques to improve the accuracy rate. Natural inspired computing (NIC) algorithms have been designed and applied to diagnose various human disorders. The authors in [3)introduced five insect-based NIC algorithms used for diagnosing diabetes and cancer. The authors found that it achieved a high level of performance in detecting different types of cancer (breast, lung, prostate and ovarian). To be more specific, breast cancer was detected using a hybridization of the guided ABC and neural networks. The authors also developed a highly effective methodology of detecting diabetes and leukemia. They concluded that the hybridization of NICs with other classification algorithms produces more precise and promising results. They mentioned that more work is required to detect different stages of diabetes and cancer.

In [4], the authors demonstrated the effectiveness of NNs in the classification of cancer diagnoses, especially in the initial stages. According to their study, the majority of NNs have shown promise in detecting tumor cells. However, the imaging approach requires high computational capacity to preprocess the images.

In [5], the authors reviewed different machine learning, deep learning and data mining algorithms related to breast cancer prediction. Several research papers on breast cancer were reviewed, with a total of 27 papers in machine learning, 4 papers in ensemble techniques and 8 papers in deep learning techniques. The authors mentioned that most of the papers used imaging, while only a few papers used genetics. The main algorithms used to predict breast cancer using genetics were SVM, decision tree and random forest. However, imaging techniques used several algorithms such as CNNs and Naïve Bayes. On the other hand, the authors

in [6] focused on gene mutation for detecting breast cancer. They mentioned that the gene prediction classification phase aims to carry out gene annotation, gene finding and gene mutation detection to ascertain the presence or absence of a cancer. They concluded that several methods can be used including regression, probability models, SVMs, NNs and deep learning. They also mentioned the many opportunities available to capture the relationship between nucleotide and feature extraction, since DNA sequencing involves a large amount of data in the form of a string sequence.

In [7], the authors examined recent studies applying deep learning to breast cancer with different imaging modalities. They organized these studies using the aspects of dataset, architecture, application and evaluation. They focused on deep learning frameworks developed in three breast imaging modalities (ultrasound, mammography and MRI). In their work, they attempted to provide state-of-the-art findings about breast cancer imaging utilizing DLR-based CAD systems. Their study included private datasets and classification using CNNs. Artificial Intelligence in Medicine, Elsevier, Vol 127, May 2022

After studying these surveys, our contribution will involve studying genetic sequencing and imaging at the same time to predict breast cancer and to get more information that can help early diagnosis and treatment of breast cancer. We will also provide recommendations to researchers who wish to conduct research in this area. 3. Methodology Our target topic is breast cancer detection using deep learning. We ended up using around 80 of the most recent papers related to breast cancer treatment and diagnosis. Some of the papers examined only deep learning, while others used a combination of machine learning and deep learning. In our search process, we mainly used the Scopus database to obtain the articles. This is to exclude nonrefereed publications However, in Figure 1, we state the distribution of selected papers among the existing databases. The top five databases are PubMed, ScienceDirect (Elsevier), IEEE, Springer and Nature.

The imaging modalities we considered were ultrasound, radiography, mammography and magnetic resonance imaging (MRI), as well as various types of gene expression and gene sequencing. In this research, we focused on papers that implement the breast cancer detection using the techniques of AI, as well as papers that predict breast cancer using both gene data and image data. We applied the following eligibility criteria on each paper: (1) The language is English; (2) The topic is related to breast cancer detection and treatment; (3) The paper discusses hybrid models of machine learning and deep learning; (4) The paper purely discusses deep learning; (5) The paper discusses genetic expression data; (6) The paper discusses imaging data; (7) Only journal and conference publications are retained; (8) Only medical or biomedical engineering publications are kept which are related to the topic. Please

note that non-refereed publications were excluded from the study. Firstly, we recorded the main information such as the name of the paper, year of publication, the list of authors and the publisher. Then, we included some information to conduct the systematic review, such as the algorithm used and whether the paper discusses only deep learning or a hybrid between DL and ML, the recorded accuracy and other performance evaluation parameters, the dataset, the features, and many other columns. We answered our research questions using these criteria. 4. Results and Discussion In this systematic study, our initial search turned up 1,000 conference and journal papers. After eliminating duplicated papers and unrelated studies that were "purely medical or about cancer in general", we ended up with 80 papers related to both ML and DL.

Printed by Libri Plureos GmbH in Hamburg,
Germany

9 798888 051016